Advanced Reading Word to Word

Various Social Issues

SHOHAKUSHA

はしがき

　地震のニュースには必ずfault「断層」という名詞が出てきますし、隣国のミサイル問題と連動してdefect「亡命する」という語もしばしば見られますが、これらを「失敗・欠点」と思って、意味を調べないで済ますならば、それは本当の失敗・欠点となります。その話題の時には必ず用いられるという頻用語句がグループで存在しています。それらを知らなくとも、知っている語句を使って発信することはできるでしょう。しかし、死傷者と行方不明を一括して表すcasualtiesを使わねば、"the killed, the injured or the missing"などと長くなるわけですし、unemployment「失業」は知っていてもunderemploymentを知らねば、派遣社員や任期付従業員、アルバイトの人たちをまとめて表すことはできません。「過労死」を外国人に説明するのに"death from overwork"で済まして通じるのでしょうか。

　編著者の私たちは大学生に30年間英語を教えてきました。その経験からはっきりわかることは、授業方針がリスニングとスピーキング中心の「コミュニケーション重視」に変わってから、積極的に英語を話す学生が増えたことです。これは誠に喜ばしい。しかし逆に、英語の語彙数が足りない、単語の綴りがあやふやな学生が増えました。試験でも英文や語句を書かせずに、マークシートや選択問題が主流ですし、単語を書いて覚えなくなったからでしょう。第１章の記事でも論じられていますが、スマートフォンで頻繁に短い語句のやり取りばかりしていることも影響しています。長い文章は敬遠する人が増えましたし、集中力も続かないのです。日本語でそうなのですから、多くの学生が長い英文を読めなくなってしまったのです。

　これは由々しき問題です。語彙力を補強しようとせず、読む力、書く力を伸ばす努力を怠っていたのでは、本当の意味での聴く力、話す力も身につきません。日本で地震を経験した外国人がしきりにaftershockについて話すのを聴いて、この人は後になってショックを受けたんだ、などと勘違いしているようではとんちんかんな会話しかできません。それこそ自分自身が後になってショックを受けることになります。語彙力こそが会話力につながるのです。そして、長い文章をストレスを感じずに読む力は、人類の学問、文化、文明を創り出していく基礎となるのです。これを侮っていては、10年後、20年後、長い目で見たときに私たちの社会は大変なことになりかねません。

　この現状を少しでも改善するために編集したのが本書です。強調されるのは、ある程度の長さの英文を最後まで読み通す気力・集中力の養成です。そこで、一つの事柄を論理的に述べるために、筋道を付けて興味深く綴るために必要な語数、平均1,000語程度の記事を集めました。これらの記事は実際に大阪大学・関西学院大学の一般英語のクラスと大学院の精読ゼミで使用した記事を主体としています。この数年間にThe Japan TimesとNikkei Asian Reviewに掲載された日本の社会問題や国際関係を報じた記事を、内容とテーマにより6章に分けました。これによって、少子高齢化や経済問題、外国人観光客の急増など、分野による重要語句や頻出表現をまとめて学習することができます。

　記事本文の前にKey Words Check「読む前に調べる重要語」を提示しました。それらの意味を辞書で確認してから、Comprehension Check「内容に関する設問」を頭に入れて、今度は辞書を使わないで記事を通読してみましょう。設問に関わる内容がどの段落に書かれていたかわかるでしょうか。2度目に読む時には、知らない語句を丁寧に辞書で調べながら、注を参考にゆっくり読んで下さい。

　学生の語彙力増強を目指す本書では、Build up Your Vocabulary「発展語彙」というセクションを設けて、各記事に出てきた語句と関連する英語表現をまとめて学習します。そして章末では、会話にも応用できるように、記事に出てきた表現を参考にして、日本の時事社会問題に関する短い英作文Current English Compositionを行ない、それら重要表現や構文の定着を図ります。これが本教科書の特長です。

　本書で英文記事をじっくりと読む習慣を身につけて、流行文化のみならず、日本の社会問題、国際関係、政治、エネルギー・自然災害対策にまで広げてほしいと思います。本書が、未来の社会を担う若い人たちに英語の文章の論理を楽しみながら読み解き、論理的に発信する力を伸ばす一助となれば、嬉しい限りです。

渡辺秀樹
大森文子

CONTENTS

I IT革命、ロボット、人間

Chapter 1	The little black screen we just can't take our eyes off スマホ中毒	5
Chapter 2	Shogi: A measure of artificial intelligence 将棋と人工知能	11
Chapter 3	Why Japan's low birth rate makes economic sense 日本の人口減少とIT革命	17

II 子供、若者、高齢者

| Chapter 4 | The high cost of peace and quiet
保育所建設と地域住民 | 23 |
| Chapter 5 | Young, old square off in a battle for the ages
若者と高齢者の対立 | 29 |

III 社会と個人

| Chapter 6 | Half a million societal drop-outs drag on Abe's economic dreams　ひきこもりの人を社会へ | 35 |
| Chapter 7 | The education system still has much to learn
いじめと教師の過労 | 41 |

IV 雇用と労働

Chapter 8	A dark force targets youth at their jobs ブラックバイト	47
Chapter 9	The unbearable burden of 24/7 work 24時間7日労働	53
Chapter 10	Debating the merits of lifetime employment 生涯雇用の消失	59

V 経済問題

Chapter 11	Disaster awaits if graying Japan delays social security reforms　高齢化の日本社会と社会保障	65
Chapter 12	Japan should tackle New Year challenges while winds are favorable　日本経済の過去と未来	71
Chapter 13	Japan's 1.2 million heirless businesses at risk of closure 後継者不足で中小企業の技術消失	77

VI 外国人と日本人

| Chapter 14 | *Omotenashi* comes up short on humility
おもてなしの心 | 83 |
| Chapter 15 | Will Japan be a country that welcomes all?
移民を受け入れるか | 89 |

▼本文出典

Chapter 1: "The little black screen we just can't take our eyes off" by Michael Hoffman, *The Japan Times* (January 15, 2017)
Chapter 2: "Shogi: A measure of artificial intelligence" by Philip Brasor, *The Japan Times* (July 9, 2017)
Chapter 3: "Why Japan's low birth rate makes economic sense" by William Collis, *The Japan Times* (November 18, 2017)
Chapter 4: "The high cost of peace and quiet" by Michael Hoffman, *The Japan Times* (July 13, 2014)
Chapter 5: "Young, old square off in a battle for the ages" by Michael Hoffman, *The Japan Times* (December 14, 2014)
Chapter 6: "Half a million societal drop-outs drag on Abe's economic dreams" by Maiko Takahashi, *The Japan Times* (November 30, 2016) / "Why Half a Million Young Japanese Can't Face School or Work" by Maiko Takahashi, *Bloomberg* (November 28, 2016). Used with permission of Bloomberg L.P. Copyright © 2017. All rights reserved.
Chapter 7: "The education system still has much to learn" by Michael Hoffman, *The Japan Times* (October 1, 2017)
Chapter 8: "A dark force targets youth at their jobs" by Philip Brasor, *The Japan Times* (October 19, 2014)
Chapter 9: "The unbearable burden of 24/7 work" by Michael Hoffman, *The Japan Times* (November 6, 2016)
Chapter 10: "Debating the merits of lifetime employment" by Philip Brasor, *The Japan Times* (November 2, 2014)
Chapter 11: "Disaster awaits if graying Japan delays social security reforms: Time to raise the pension eligibility age and share the health insurance burden more equally", *Nikkei Asian Review* (May 8, 2018)
Chapter 12: "Japan should tackle New Year challenges while winds are favorable: Time is ripe to address such issues as labor reforms and social security spending", *Nikkei Asian Review* (January 11, 2018)
Chapter 13: "Japan's 1.2 million heirless businesses at risk of closure: With 'Rolls Royce' of chalk already gone, country could lose key technologies" by Takashi Tsuji, *Nikkei Asian Review* (October 9, 2017)
Chapter 14: "'Omotenashi' comes up short on humility" by Philip Brasor, *The Japan Times* (October 11, 2015)
Chapter 15: "Will Japan be a country that welcomes all?" by Michael Hoffman, *The Japan Times* (May 25, 2014)

Chapter 1

スマホ中毒

皆さんが一日にスマートフォンの画面を見る時間はどれくらいですか。使いすぎて疲れていませんか。スマートフォンの情報をどの程度信じていますか。スマートフォンとの付き合い方についてあらためて考えてみましょう。

Ⅰ ーＴ革命、ロボット、人間

Key Words Check

これから読む記事に登場する重要単語をチェックしましょう。
（　）内は該当する段落番号を示しています。

- insomnia (3)
- inundation (3)
- swindle (3)
- ubiquitous (4)
- begrudge (5)
- concoct (9)
- eyestrain (10)
- avalanche (11)
- paltry (12)

The little black screen we just can't take our eyes off

CD1 02

1 A great weight sits perched on us. It's called a head. It houses our brain and presents our face to the world. It comprises roughly 10 percent of our body weight. Heavy enough at the best of times, it grows heavier as it inclines forward. Held high, it's a 5.5-kilogram burden on the neck of a person who weighs 55 kg. Bent forward 15 degrees, the burden becomes the equivalent of 12.2 kg; 30 degrees, 18.1 kg; 45 degrees, 22.2 kg; 60 degrees, 27.2 kg.

2 Lately more and more people are bending farther and farther forward, peering ever more intently into a tiny screen packed solid with ever more irresistible attractions. We are speaking—or rather, the weekly magazine Spa! is speaking—of smartphones. Its package of articles, from which the above data are extracted, is titled "The tragedy of smartphone addiction."

3 A slouching posture is hardly the worst of it. Smartphone abuse, we are told, rots the brain, dims the eyesight, heightens anxiety, feeds insomnia, dulls thought, trivializes communication, distorts our view of the world with an inundation of false and/or shallow information, takes up ruinous amounts of time, and makes us prey to all kinds of insidious swindles, most notably in the form of PR dressed up as fact.

4 Japan was relatively slow to embrace the smartphone, but initial hesitation is a fading memory, and now, here as elsewhere, the device is ubiquitous and all but inescapable. Spa! does not precisely define "addiction." Figure, it says, three hours plus of daily use. Among the "addicts" it interviews is one who was appalled to discover—via an app that clocks use—that he spends six hours a day clicking here, clicking there, viewing this, checking that; nothing special, but it all adds up—without, in his apparently exceptional case, impairing his professional or family life.

5 Others sense something decidedly wrong, but momentum propels them onward—to seven hours a day in one case, 10 in another. "Ozawa-san," the seven-hour-a-day man, is obsessed with points. Visiting certain sites, and doing certain things on them—participating in surveys, for example, or using certain search engines—earns you points. Points are convertible into cash. Ozawa, an engineer not hurting for money, finds nonetheless a satisfaction in earning points that earning a salary, routine and predictable, denies. He collects point after point; in a year they're worth ¥600,000. He begrudges the attention his job demands: "I can't help thinking as I work, 'How many points could I be earning now?'"

6 "Tsuda-san" spends 10 hours a day gaming. "Mobile Strike" is a special favorite: "I started playing in March and got hooked." At work he games in the toilet whenever possible. Home from the office at 8 p.m., he's at his phone by 9—until 3 a.m., which gives him three hours' sleep, when he can sleep at all. He dozes at his desk. It's not the life he'd choose. It seems to have chosen him.

7 Similarly, Line, the charge-free message app, seems to have chosen "Yasugawa-san." Even at no cost, 600 messages a day seems like a lot.

---

incline:（物が）傾く、傾斜する

peer into：～をのぞき込む

→ 📖 1
slouching：前屈みの、猫背の

distort：（真実などを）ゆがめる

Unfortunately, "my idiot boss" is fixated on it, which means Yasugawa must be, too. Line etiquette does not permit replying later to messages received now. A reply is either instant, or it's an offense. If that's true among friends, how much the more so with your boss?

8 Such, Spa! sums up sardonically, are the blessings of modern civilization.

9 There are other, less dark—even bright—views of the smartphone. The Asahi Shimbun, in its Coming-of-Age Day editorial last week, termed the youngest members of the adult community "the smartphone generation"—the first to come of age with the device, taking it for granted as their grandparents did television, their great-grandparents radio. The editorial praised Line and other social networking services for bringing people together, promoting free expression, culture, creativity —all good things, surely; but all good things, embraced too eagerly, bite the hand that strokes them. Yasugawa seems to find Line's togetherness more stifling than fraternal. As for free expression, one is free to express oneself and spread the truth as one sees it, and no less free to concoct, spread and believe, for example, that Pope Francis endorsed Donald Trump for president of the United States, the fact that he did no such thing being more or less beside the point. Never has it been easier to express truth or spread falsehood; never has it been more difficult to distinguish between the two. Never have so few people wanted to.

10 "Brain in danger," reads a smartphone screen in one of Spa!'s illustrations. For expert testimony the magazine turns to Waseda University neurologist Yoshikuni Edagawa. He begins by discussing the "blue light problem." All computers emit high-energy, short-wave blue light. Smartphones, held particularly close to the eye, are especially conducive to the eyestrain associated with it. Eyestrain and consequent visual deterioration are symptoms frequently noted. Less so is another effect of blue light: it inhibits the hormone melatonin, thus obstructing sleep. Insomnia affects different people differently. Some can live more or less normally with it. Others can't, and their behavior in consequence can be less responsible than is good for themselves and society at large.

11 Short-term memory loss is another concern Edagawa raises. The rapid succession of facts and images bombarding the chronic smartphone user are more than the brain can absorb. Memory gives way under the avalanche. "What if it does?" Edagawa fears you might say—"my smartphone can remember anything I can't." "It's not too much to say," he sums up, "that smartphone abuse will make you stupid."

12 Does even that matter? If smartphones are smart, so what if we're not? Then there's the much bruited "singularity" just around the corner: by 2045 or thereabouts, say some experts, computer intelligence will begin to make human intelligence in general, not just yours or mine, seem paltry and, finally, irrelevant. That, too, to paraphrase Spa! once more, is "a blessing of modern civilization."

(1015 words)

Comprehension Check

1 本文では、ポイントサイトでお金を稼ぐ人の話が出てきますが、この人のポイント稼ぎの動機は何でしょうか。まとめなさい。

2 第6段落末尾は "It seems to have chosen him." という文で締めくくられ、第7段落冒頭は "Similarly, Line, the charge-free message app, seems to have chosen 'Yasugawa-san.'" という文で始まりますが、これらはどのような事象を表していますか。それぞれについてまとめなさい。

3 第9段落末尾の "Never has it been easier to express truth or spread falsehood; never has it been more difficult to distinguish between the two. Never have so few people wanted to." という記述はどのようなことを述べようとしていますか。解説しなさい。

4 この記事で多出する比喩表現を集めて、その使い方を考えましょう。
Ex. Memory gives way under the avalanche.（第 11 段落）

Build up Your Vocabulary

1

第 3 段落で "Smartphone abuse"「スマホ中毒」という表現がありました。関連して、以下の日本語の意味を表す英語表現を確認しましょう。

児童虐待

薬物濫用

職権濫用

人権侵害

2

第 9 段落で fraternal「（男）兄弟の」という形容詞がありますが、「親の」「父親の」「母親の」「姉妹の」「配偶者の」の意味の形容詞を確認しましょう。

Helpful Notes

1 ▷ 『週刊 Spa!』（2016 年 12 月 27 日号）では「みんなバカになる！『スマホ中毒』の悲劇」と題された特集記事が組まれ、スマートフォンが人間に及ぼす深刻な影響に焦点を当てている。

2 ▷ これは "bite the hand which feeds one"「恩を仇で返す・世話になった人を裏切る」の意味で犬を意味上の主語とする固定表現のもじり。

3 ▷ この avalanche「雪崩」は数行前の "the rapid succession" の言い換えの比喩表現。第 3 段落 "an inundation of false and/or shallow information" も「洪水」の意味の名詞を多量を意味する比喩で用いていることを参照。激しい気象を意味する名詞は「連続・殺到」の意味で比喩的に用いられる。a blizzard of laws「続けざまに成立した法律」。

4 ▷ singularity とは米国の発明家レイ・カーツワイル（1948-）が提唱した概念で、人工知能が人類の知能を超える転換点（技術的特異点）を指す。コンピュータ技術の発達が一定の度合いを超えると、人工知能が人間の制御を凌駕し、人間の生活を恐ろしいまでに変容させてしまう。この転換点が 2045 年に到来する、という仮説である。

Current English Composition

次の日本語を英語にしなさい。
ただし、下線を引いた部分は下線部のみを英語にしなさい。

1 消費者市場のもう一つの重要な変化は、退職する人々がどんどん増えているこの状況で、日本の社会が高齢化していることである。
（第2段落 "more and more people are bending" 参考）

Another significant change in the consumer market is the graying of Japanese society as _____
_____ .

2 広く世界を見渡す政治家やビジネスリーダーは、自国でのやり方がいつも外国で通用すると考えてはならない。（第4段落 elsewhere 参考）

Outward-looking politicians and business leaders should know that _____
_____
_____ .

3 （ロンドンオリンピックに向けて）殺到する観光客に対応するために現在ヨーロッパで最大規模の地下鉄の駅が建設中であるが、この広大な場所がかつてはロンドンの汚染された河岸地域であったことを想像できる人はいない。
（第11段落 "rapid succession of facts and images…the avalanche" 参考）

The largest underground station in Europe is being built _____
_____ , who will never imagine that the large area was once London's polluted riverside site.

4 私たちは皆、十分に睡眠が取れていないと思っているが、日本人は世界の中でも、特によく眠れない国民なのである。（第10段落 "obstructing sleep…Insomnia" 参考）

We all worry that we're not getting enough sleep. _____
_____ .

Chapter 2 将棋と人工知能

Ⅰ ─ IT革命、ロボット、人間

公式戦連勝の新記録を樹立した天才棋士、藤井聡太七段の活躍に日本中が大いに沸き、将棋ブームが到来しました。彼の強さの秘密はどこにあるのでしょうか。また、これまで伝統的で地味という印象を持たれていた将棋が、なぜこれほどの注目を集めているのでしょうか。

©時事

Key Words Check

これから読む記事に登場する重要単語をチェックしましょう。
（ ）内は該当する段落番号を示しています。

- assembly (1)
- vanguard (2)
- daily (4)
- artificial intelligence (5)
- exonerate (8)
- exponentially (9)
- hopeful (11)
- leapfrog (11)

Shogi: A measure of artificial intelligence

1 Though last Sunday's Tokyo assembly elections garnered the most media attention, another contest came in a close second, even if only two people were involved. Fourteen-year-old Sota Fujii's record-setting winning streak of 29 games of shogi was finally broken on July 2 when he lost a match to 22-year-old Yuki Sasaki.

2 Fujii has turned into a media superstar in the past year because of his youth and exceptional ability in a game that non-enthusiasts may find too cerebral to appreciate. The speed of Fujii's ascension to headline status has been purposely accelerated by the media, which treats him as not just a prodigy, but as the vanguard figure of a pastime in which the media has a stake.

3 Press photos of Fujii's matches show enormous assemblies of reporters, video crews and photographers hovering over the kneeling opponents. Such attention may seem ridiculous to some people owing to the solemnity surrounding shogi, which is played much like chess, but if Fujii succeeds in attracting new fans, then the media is all for it.

4 That's because all the national dailies and some broadcasters cover shogi regularly and in detail. In fact, most major shogi tournaments are sponsored by media outlets. The Ryuo Sen championship, toward which Fujii was aiming when he lost last week, is the biggest in terms of prize money, and is sponsored by the Yomiuri Shimbun. NHK also has a tournament and airs a popular shogi instructional program several times a week.

5 The Fujii fuss, however, is about more than his prodigal skills. Fujii ushers an old game with a stuffy image into the present by accommodating the 21st century's most fickle god: artificial intelligence. Much has been made in the past few weeks of Fujii's style of play, which is described as being counter-intuitive and abnormally aggressive. What almost all the critics agree on is that he honed this style through self-training that involved the use of dedicated shogi software incorporating AI.

6 But before Fujii's revolutionary strategic merits could be celebrated, AI needed to be accepted, and a scandal last July put such technology into focus. One of the top players in the game, Hiroyuki Miura, was accused by his opponent of cheating after he won a match. Miura repeatedly left the room during play and was suspected of consulting his phone when he did so. The Japan Shogi Association (JSA) suspended him as they investigated the charges.

7 As outlined by Toru Takeda in the Nov. 22 online version of Asahi Shimbun, the JSA checked the moves Miura had made in previous games against moves made by popular shogi software to see if there was a pattern. In four of his victories there was a 90 percent rate of coincidence. Miura's smartphone was also checked by a third party, which found no shogi app. Moreover, there was no communications activity recorded for the phone on the day of the contested match because it had been shut off the whole time.

8 Miura was officially exonerated on May 24, at the height of the media's "Sota fever," but that doesn't mean Miura was not using shogi software to change his game strategy. In November last year, Takeda theorized that, given the prevalence of the software and the amount of progress programmers had made in improving its AI functions, it's impossible to believe that there is a professional shogi player who has not yet taken advantage of the technology. Miura, he surmised, had become what chess grandmaster Garry Kasparov once called a "centaur"—half man, half computerized beast. By studying the way shogi programs played, Miura had likely appropriated the AI function's own learning curve. He didn't have to check the software to determine moves—it was already in his nervous system. Miura is, in fact, one of the pros who battled computerized shogi programs in past years. In 2013, he played against shogi software developed by the University of Tokyo and lost.

9 The evolution of shogi software was covered in a recent NHK documentary about AI. Amahiko Sato, one of the game's highest ranked players, has played the shogi robot Ponanza several times without a victory. The robot's programmer told NHK that he input 20 years of moves by various professionals into the program and it has since been playing itself. Since computers decide at a speed that is exponentially faster than humans, the software has played itself about 7 million times, learning more with each game.

10 "It's like using a shovel to compete with a bulldozer," Yoshiharu Habu, Japan's top shogi player, commented to NHK after describing Ponanza's moves as "unbelievable."

11 Fujii is simply the human manifestation of this evolution, and what's disconcerting for the shogi establishment is that he didn't reach that position because of a mentor. As with most skills in Japan, shogi hopefuls usually learn by sitting at the feet of masters and copying their technique in a rote fashion until they've developed it into something successful and idiosyncratic. Fujii leapfrogged the mentor phase thanks to shogi software.

12 An article in the June 27 Asahi Shimbun identified Shota Chida as the player who turned Fujii on to AI a year ago, just before Fujii turned pro. On the NHK program Habu noticed something significant as a result: Fujii's moves became faster and more decisive. He achieved victory with fewer moves by abandoning the conventional strategy of building a defense before going on the offensive. Fujii constantly looks for openings in his opponent's game and immediately strikes when he sees one, which is the main characteristic of AI shogi.

13 Fujii's defeat obviously means that his type of play is no longer confounding. Masataka Sugimoto, his shogi teacher, told Tokyo Shimbun that he doesn't think Fujii "uses software as a weapon," since he now faces players who also practiced with AI. But that doesn't mean his game play hasn't been changed by AI. Before the Miura scandal, pros who used software were considered the board-game equivalents of athletes who took performance-enhancing drugs. Now they're the norm, and the media couldn't be happier.

(1010 words)

Comprehension Check

1 世間の注目を集める藤井聡太氏の棋士としての特徴はどこにありますか。まとめなさい。

2 将棋界の上層部の人々が不安を感じているのは藤井聡太氏のどのような点ですか。

3 記事の最終文 "Now they're the norm, and the media couldn't be happier" を日本語に訳し、本文の内容から見て、なぜこのような結論になっているのか、あなたの考えを述べなさい。

Build up Your Vocabulary

1

本文第4段落に daily「日刊紙」という表現がありました。以下の意味を表す英語表現を覚えましょう。

月刊誌

季刊誌

隔週刊行誌

年刊

2

第11段落には hopefuls「前途有望な若者」という語がありましたが、「〜を目指している人」の意の類似表現にはどのような表現がありますか。形容詞について調べましょう。

I T革命、ロボット、人間

Helpful Notes

1 ▷ これまでは竜王、名人、棋聖、王将、王座、棋王、王位の7大タイトル戦であったが、叡王戦が格上げされて現在は8大タイトル。

2 ▷ NHK 教育チャンネルでは日曜10時30分から早指しの将棋トーナメント、12時30分から囲碁トーナメントを放映し、先立つ30分間にそれぞれの解説番組を放映している。

3 ▷ 「偶然の」の類語に accidental, unintended, 反義「故意に、意図的な」には on purpose, deliberate, intentional などがある。

4 ▷ こうした世間の見方に対しては、藤井の師匠杉本昌隆七段の見解を参考にすべきである。「藤井について「AI（人工知能）棋士」という表現をされることがあります。「時代の申し子」という意味でしょうか。少し違うなと感じます。彼がここまで強くなった背景には詰将棋で培った地道な努力があり、人との対戦で身につけた感性や勝負術があります。これはきわめてアナログ的なものです。」（杉本昌隆著『弟子・藤井聡太の学び方』PHP出版 p. 81）。第13段落の杉本七段の発言引用の英文と比較。

5 ▷ 藤井聡太は2018年には2月1日に順位戦で勝利して昇組するとともに五段となり、2月17日には朝日杯準決勝で羽生善治竜王に勝ち、決勝で広瀬章人八段に勝って初の棋戦優勝、六段昇段。中学生棋士の五段・六段昇段は史上初。次いで3月8日の王将戦第1次予選で師匠の杉本七段と対戦し、これにも勝利。5月18日には第31期竜王戦5組ランキング戦準決勝で船江恒平六段に勝って、竜王戦4組に昇級。史上最年少15歳9カ月で七段に昇進した。これまでの最年少記録は加藤一二三九段の「17歳3カ月」であった。2017年度は将棋界にとって空前の年となった。藤井の29連勝の新記録に加え、加藤一二三九段の引退と「ひふみん」という流行語、ポーランド人、カロリーナ・ステチャンスカが外国人初の女流プロ棋士となり、佐藤天彦名人がコンピュータソフトに負けた。叡王戦が昇格して34年ぶりに新タイトル戦ができて8大タイトルになった。藤井は2017年度の勝率・勝利数・対局数・連勝の部門で四冠。

Current English Composition

次の日本語を英語にしなさい。
ただし、下線を引いた部分は下線部のみを英語にしなさい。

1 日本のプロの囲碁棋士井山裕太は、初めて七冠を達成した（7大タイトルを同時に取得した）。

2 昨年10月1日現在、日本の人口は0.17%減って、1億2千730万人になったが、注目すべきは、この国が世界で最も低い出生率であることだ。人口の4分の1以上が今や65歳以上の高齢者である。（第11段落 "what's disconcerting for the shogi establishment is that he didn't reach that position because of a mentor." 参考）

As of October 1 last year, Japan's population has decreased by .17% to 127.3 million. _____ .
A quarter of the country's total population is made up of people 65 or older.

3 ユネスコが和食（日本食）を世界無形文化遺産に指定したが、このニュースは、批判の的になっていた外食業界にとって、またとない良いタイミングで訪れた。
（第13段落 Now they're the norm, and the media couldn't be happier. 参考）

UNESCO formally recognized Japanese cuisine, *washoku*, as part of the world's Intangible Cultural Heritage. _____
_____ .

4 機械は今や様々な競技で人間を打ち負かしている。テレビのクイズ番組やチェス、最近では、機械が習得できるとは思われなかった戦略を必要とするゲームである囲碁においてもそうだ。

Machines now beat humans in various competitions, from TV quiz shows (like "Jeopardy") to chess and most recently go, _____
_____ .

Chapter 3

日本の人口減少とIT革命

少子高齢化が加速している日本社会は、人口減少という大きな問題に直面していますが、この記事では、人口減少には必ずしも悪い面ばかりではなく、意外に良い面もあるということが述べられています。変わりゆく社会情勢の中で、日本は人口減少とどう向き合い、社会の発展のために人口動態をどのように生かしていけば良いのでしょうか。

Key Words Check

これから読む記事に登場する重要単語をチェックしましょう。
（ ）内は該当する段落番号を示しています。

- labor force (1)
- exacerbate (1)
- unemployment (3)
- commuter train (6)
- catalyze (7)
- economic power (7)
- life expectancy (9)
- circuitously (9)
- reductio ad absurdum (11)

Why Japan's low birth rate makes economic sense

1 PROVIDENCE, RHODE ISLAND – Japan's low birth rate is often framed as the definitive crisis facing the country. A shrinking population constricts the labor force, drives economic stagnation, exacerbates elderly care costs, and eventually leads to cultural collapse. But is this actually true? I argue that Japan's shrinking population is not all bad, and may actually present a hidden advantage to navigating this century's artificial intelligence revolution.

2 To begin, I'd like to address the argument typically presented against Japan's current demographic trends. Broadly, Japan is believed to be experiencing a collective action problem. While it may make sense for individual families to have few or no children due to monetary and temporal constraints, collectively the country as a whole should want more kids. Therefore, government policies are needed to incent childbirth — which we see implemented today with middling efficacy.

3 But why should Japan want more children? The obvious, direct consequence of a lower birth rate is a constricting labor supply. But fewer workers is not necessarily a bad thing. Thinning labor puts upward pressure on wages, increasing living standards and reducing unemployment. In fact, reducing the labor supply is the rationale commonly given (though arguably justified) for reducing immigration in my home country of the United States. The counterbalancing risk, of course, is that expensive labor makes Japanese products less competitive, reducing exports and shrinking GDP.

4 But this downside is only true if labor cannot be effectively substituted with technology. And there is very good reason to believe that not just the Japanese—but the global labor force—is due for a massive labor substitution. Advances in artificial intelligence (AI) and automation will eliminate between 30 percent to 60 percent of today's jobs, depending on which major study you prefer. Positions like trucking, cashiering and clerking will be first to go; but even relatively skilled jobs like paralegals and analysts are predicted to be lost within two decades.

5 Given this massive technological shift, a reduced birth rate makes anticipatory sense. In the U.S., futurists like the firm Y-Combinator are advocating for a universal basic human income to address social instability due to spiking unemployment. But in Japan, the labor supply is preemptively thinning. The reasons behind Japan's low birthrate may not necessarily be healthy—overly demanding jobs, lack of institutional support for families, and more—but that does not mean the outcome of these factors is wholly undesirable.

6 And there may be other, unanticipated benefits to a shrinking Japan. The country's population is three times the size of California's—packed in a significantly smaller land mass. Compounding crowding is Japan's mountainous terrain, which covers over 70 percent of the country. Population thinning may reduce congestion in cities, render urban housing more affordable, and even ease crowding on Japan's packed commuter trains.

incent：奨励する、incentivize の短形

paralegal：弁護士補助員

preemptively：前もって、あらかじめ予想して

7 Finally, a reduction in Japan's population may ultimately catalyze necessary societal reform. Already Japan's low birthrate is prompting limited immigration reform, making it easier for certain categories of foreigners to live and work in the country. Japan is not self-destructive; it stands to reason that if population shrinkage continues, Japan will increasingly modernize its immigration policies. Ultimately, labor market forces may incite Japan to open up in a way inconceivable to the country now, but vital to its continued success as an economic power.

8 So what are the downsides to Japan's low birthrate? The two most typically cited are burdensome elderly care, and weakening national security. Let's look at each in turn.

9 As global life expectancy increases, the costs of caring for the elderly will naturally rise in most major economies. It is not the rising cost of elderly care by itself that's the problem, but the per-capita burden of these costs. An aging population isn't bad if the productive workforce remains large proportionally. And in Japan, this just might be the case. The retirement age is projected to rise to 65 in the next few years; as major companies recognize older employees can still contribute to the workforce. And human-centered jobs like elderly care are cited as some of the best insulated against AI displacement. Almost circuitously, an older population may prove a source of employment.

10 What about national security, and Japan's reduced ability to protect itself? Here again the coming technology revolution might suggest this is not as much of a problem as it seems. I believe the interdependent nature of today's largest economies makes direct conflict unlikely, and even then Japan is bulwarked by its military relationship with the U.S. And if you believe, like I do, that digital warfare, IP-theft and cybercrimes are likely the battlefields of tomorrow, then a shrinking population simply reduces the surface area of the target.

11 The arguments presented here are intentionally overstated for the sake of brevity. I do not believe that a shrinking population is an unequivocal good. For example, I am particularly concerned about the cultural risks to Japan, and Japan's diminishing influence abroad. And taken reductio ad absurdum, a declining population threatens the end of Japan itself. My point is chiefly that the coming technology shift means our old assumptions about human capital and domestic productivity do not necessarily hold.

12 Ultimately, I would prefer Japan to have a higher birthrate — like most rational thinkers. But I also try to look on the bright side of the population chasm. As AI eliminates traditional employment, Japan may actually be well-positioned to safely navigate its transition.

(960 words)

Comprehension Check

1 第2段落に見られる "collective action problem" とは、どのような問題ですか。この概念について調べ、本文では具体的にどのような事象を指しているか説明しなさい。

2 第5段落冒頭の "this massive technological shift" とはどのような事象を表していますか。具体的に説明しなさい。

3 この記事の筆者の論旨における人口減少を続ける日本の有利な点を、150字程度の日本語で要約しなさい。

Build up Your Vocabulary

1

第3段落に unemployment「失業」という言葉があります。この語に関連して雇用関連の以下の日本語に相当する英語表現を調べましょう。

正規雇用

非正規雇用（不十分雇用）

有給休暇

忌引き

2

第7段落終わりに an economic power「経済大国」、第9段落に major economies「主要国」という表現があります。これに関連して、以下の意味で、country, nation などの名詞を用いない英語表現を調べましょう。

超大国

欧州列強

海洋大国

宇宙開発国

新興国

アジアの民主国

3

この記事では高齢者のケアの問題が論じられていました。高齢化社会で増えて行く現象を表す以下の意味の英語表現を調べましょう。

認知症

徘徊老人

孤独死

介護保険

高齢者福祉施設

Helpful Notes

1 ▷ 名詞の前に対比的・対照的意味の形容詞が2つ並ぶ時には、2つの間に接続詞 and を置くか、その代わりにコンマで区切る。

2 ▷ 「意味がわかる、納得できる」というような意味で使われる連語 "make sense" の間に形容詞が置かれる形。"It also makes political sense for Mr. Trump to give a nod to religious voters."「トランプ大統領が、キリスト教を信じている人々を応援するという態度を見せたのは、政治的な効果を狙った行為としてうなずける」というように使われる。

3 ▷ 国名、都市名や人名などの固有名詞に冠詞（a, the）が付く場合がある。映画の中で描かれたパリ、時代小説の中の江戸時代の日本など。ここでは現在の日本ではなく、数十年後に人口が減ったと想定される日本を指す。

4 ▷ p. 90 Chapter 15 第2段落の "economic superpower" 参照。

5 ▷ 経済の話をしている時には名詞 economy が「（独立した一つの）経済圏としての国」の意で頻用される。同様に、文化や政治体制に言及する culture や democracy も、しばしば国を意味して使われる。

Current English Composition

次の日本語を英語にしなさい。
ただし、下線を引いた部分は下線部のみを英語にしなさい。

1. 周りの国々のことをしっかり考えるような日本は、アジアの将来を指導できる、指導すべき国になるだろう。

2. <u>本大学の学部生に、被災地でボランティア活動に参加することを課すのは教育的意味があるのでしょうか。</u>（Title の "makes economic sense" や第 5 段落の "makes anticipatory sense" の形容詞の用法を参考に）

   _____
   _____ that require (taking part in) volunteer activities in the disaster-hit areas?

3. 認知症（老人性痴呆症）は現在日本で深刻な社会的問題を起こしている。<u>認知症の老人は、一日の多くの時間を通りを、徘徊して過ごすこともあり、それを見ている人は彼らが助けを必要としているとは気付かない。</u>

   Senile dementia is causing serious social problems in Japan. _____
   _____
   without anyone knowing they are in need of help.

4. <u>世界で最も急速に高齢化した長寿国である</u>日本は、近く到来する世界的健康管理危機の先端にいる。

   _____
   _____ , Japan is at the forefront of an impending global health crisis.

Chapter 4
保育所建設と地域住民

子育てをしながら働く親を支援するには保育所・託児所が必要です。少子化を憂いつつも自分たちの静寂が脅かされると考えて、保育所建設に反対する地域住民もいます。どのように解決できるでしょうか。

II 子供、若者、高齢者

Key Words Check

これから読む記事に登場する重要単語をチェックしましょう。
（　）内は該当する段落番号を示しています。

- clamorous (2)
- hectic (4)
- crusty (5)
- upscale (8)
- reactionary (8)
- aground (9)
- edgy (10)
- morass (12)

The high cost of peace and quiet

1 Peace and quiet! How rare it is, how precious. Why rare? Because a full-blooded modern economy is no monastery, no "ancient pond" into which a frog may jump, producing the hushed "sound of water" immortalized by the haiku poet Basho (1644-94).

2 Engines roar, machinery hums, advertisements blare. Try getting away from it. Maybe, just maybe, if you live in a quiet neighborhood, if your walls are thick, if you're not too near a train station or construction site or compulsively barking dogs or convenience store parking lot or main road over which trucks thunder, you can shut your door against the clamorous chaos of the outside world, close your eyes and sink—until the outside world summons you forth again, as it all too soon will—into that blessed state called silence.

3 It's not obvious yet, but this story is about children. What's the connection? Well, they're noisy. They can't help it. They shout with joy, wail with sorrow. Everything's a big deal to them. Self-restraint is not in their nature, bless them. Adults must make the best of it. It helps, in strained moments when that seems impossible, to recall that you too, after all, were once a child.

4 Now suppose this: You've got your thick walls and your quiet neighborhood, having sacrificed a considerable portion of your income for them—peace and quiet is not cheap! Ah, but it's worth it. What joy, what relief, to come home at the end of a hectic, frenetic, distracted—that is to say, normal—day and enter a different world, a hushed world, the *real* world!

5 Or perhaps you're retired and spend most of your time at home; perhaps you live alone, and solitude and the passing years have made you a bit crusty: You tire easily, are not as patient as you once were. It's a fault, to be sure. You would amend it if you could, but after all, your home is your castle—your monastery, even. If you can't be your own genuine, flawed self here, where can you be?

6 Suddenly plans are announced to build a day care center right in your neighborhood—for 80, 100, 120 kids. Is it mean-spirited to feel that your little world has been blasted to smithereens? No doubt it is. You are aware, as everyone is, how important day care is. Japan needs working women, and it needs children. Without day care it can have one or the other—not both. So day care centers must be built. But why *here*? Why just where *I* happen to live?

7 Well, they have to be somewhere. Prime Minister Shinzo Abe, acknowledging a dire shortage, has promised day care accommodation for an additional 400,000 children by 2017.

8 Day care operators, established and would-be, are rising to the challenge. So are local residents—with massive protests. In an upscale neighborhood in Tokyo's Shinagawa Ward, Aera magazine reported in April, 1,700 residents in the immediate vicinity of a planned three-story facility for 90 children signed a petition against it. To working mothers desperate for relief, this smacks of a reactionary inability to change with the times. "People around here think mothers should stay home with their kids all day long," grumbles the 39-year-old mother of a 6-year-old.

9 There's that, but also more. The women's weekly Shukan Josei finds Shinagawa echoing far afield. In Fukuoka, a planned center for 120 children ran aground against local opposition. The company behind it did its best. It held meeting after meeting with residents—seven altogether. You're worried about noise? We'll install soundproofing. You're afraid our kids will take over the local park? We'll send them out in small groups, and clean up after them. And so on and so on.

10 No dice. The locals weren't buying. Finally, the company pulled out. Better safe than sorry. There are cautionary examples of what might have been in store for it had it proceeded. In Saitama, neighbors are up in arms against an existing day care center. Noise, first of all. The center installed double windows and air conditioning. Better, but not good enough. Then there were the curry smells wafting from the day care kitchen chimney. The center put in a filter. Another problem: Women were edgy about their drying laundry being in plain view of kids playing on the day care center roof. The center put up a fence. On and on it went—and goes.

11 It can end up in court. One in Tokyo is currently hearing a suit by residents to the effect that a neighborhood day care center "violates their right to a quiet life."

12 Is there such a right in today's society? If so, day care centers are hardly the worst offenders. Let the reader draw up his or her own personal list of pet nuisances in this crowded, cheek-by-jowl country, and then think how swamped the courts will be if they get dragged into this morass. And yet, the "right to a quiet life" does seem somehow an essential part of civilization, whatever its standing in law might be.

13 Meanwhile in Osaka, Shukan Josei reports, residents last year told a company planning a day care center in their area that they'd drop their opposition—providing the company paid annual compensation for the inconveniences that would inevitably result. No thanks, said the company, giving up at last.

14 So who wins this tug of war between the individual's rights and society's claims? No one, so far.

(990 words)

waft：ただよう、類語 drift, float

nuisance：不愉快なこと、迷惑
swamp：水浸しにする、沈める

Comprehension Check

1 本記事には中心概念となる neighborhood が繰り返し出てきます。どのような意味・用法があるかを辞書で確認し、この記事での意味を考えなさい。接尾辞の –hood についても意味を確認して、書き出しなさい。

2 第 10 段落の表現 "Better safe than sorry" の表すところを、記事の前後の文脈から説明しなさい。

3 第 12 段落で、裁判沙汰になった託児所問題を効果的な比喩表現で表しています。これについて各自の考えを述べなさい。

Build up Your Vocabulary

1

第2段落で "Engines roar, machinery hums, advertisements blare." と、動物の鳴き声を表す動詞が連続して比喩用法で使われています。これと関連して、犬や猫の鳴き声を表す以下の動詞が、人間に対して用いられた時に、どのような比喩義を持つか調べましょう。

bark　　　　yap
growl　　　mew
howl　　　　purr

2

第6段落に "mean-spirited"「卑しい心を持った」という表現がありますが、このように名詞に接尾辞 –ed が付くと所有の意味の形容詞になります。以下の意味でこの形式の形容詞を含む英語表現を確認しましょう。

有能な作曲家
羽のある生き物
多面的研究
優しい心を持った紳士
3階建ての家

3

第7段落に a dire shortage「ひどい不足」という連語がありますが、程度のはなはだしさを意味する形容詞と、それが修飾する名詞とは、意味関係によって自然な連結パターンがあります。次の「欠乏・不足」を意味する名詞を頻繁に修飾する形容詞を調べましょう。

loss
lack
ignorance
absence

Helpful Notes

1 ▷ full-blooded「血気盛んな、充実した」cf. sanguine, anemic
2 ▷ "An Englishman's home is his castle"「英国人の家は城」という諺のもじり。究極的にはラテン語の "et domus sua cuique est tutissimum refugium (and each man's home is his safest refuge)"「家とは逃げ場所」に遡ることも参照。続く monastery「修道院」は、中世の宗教組織で俗世間と離れて僧が多弁を避け、瞑想・祈り・作業に没頭する場所。日本なら禅寺修行僧の静謐な生活に相当。
3 ▷ この構文は finds / Shinagawa / echoing far afield「品川の託児所問題が遠く（福岡）で反響したのを見つけた」と取る。
4 ▷ この "better safe than sorry" は、"better late than never"「遅くなってもやらないよりまし」、"better early than late"「思い立ったが吉日」などの諺の形を模した頭韻表現であること注意。
5 ▷ to the effect that...「...という趣旨の」手紙の内容や申し立てについて使う表現。
6 ▷ ここでの standing は法律用語の「原告適格、訴訟を提起できる正当な資格・権利」の意味であるが、先行する morass などから「足場」の意味が掛けてあると思われる。

Current English Composition

次の日本語を英語にしなさい。
ただし、下線を引いた部分は下線部のみを英語にしなさい。

1 現在、深刻な人手不足に直面している日本の建設業界は、実は、何年も前から規模が縮小してきている。（第 7 段落 a dire shortage 参考）

_____

_____ has in fact been shrinking for years.

2 その政策は日本の都合だけを考えていると匂わせるもので、目論まれた利益よりも、かえって問題をたくさん引き起こすかもしれない。（第 8 段落 smacks of 参考）

_____

_____ , it could cause problems that outweigh the intended benefits.

3 日本では 2040 年に約 77 万トン相当のソーラーパネルが役立った寿命を終えて廃棄される見込みである。（第 11 段落 end up 参考）

About 770,000 tons worth of solar panels _____

_____

_____ .

4 日本で保証されている産休の期間は、出産予定日の前の 6 週間と出産後の 8 週間です。

_____

six weeks before the expected birth date and eight weeks after giving birth.

Chapter 5

若者と高齢者の対立

高齢者は急増し、出生率の低下から若者の数は減っています。元気で自立している多くのお年寄りは頼もしいですが、認知症の増加、暴力を振るったり礼儀に欠けると思われる高齢者も増えました。どうすれば良いのでしょうか。

II　子供、若者、高齢者

© Sarawut Aiemsinsuk / Shutterstock.com

Key Words Check

これから読む記事に登場する重要単語をチェックしましょう。
（　）内は該当する段落番号を示しています。

- blasé (4)
- delivery (5)
- dementia (6)
- defiance (6)
- perpetrate (7)
- gnash one's teeth (8)
- come of age (8)
- centenarian (13)

Young, old square off in a battle for the ages

1 You'd think they owned the planet. *They* think they do—pushing into line at supermarkets, hogging seats on trains, generally behaving as though no one but themselves existed except to provide the services they need.

2 Once upon a time—not very long ago—that was how the old talked about the young. Now, it's the young tweeting about the old. In both cases, the subtext is, "Have they no shame?" And the answer, in both cases, is, "Not at all; they have pride."

3 Once upon a time—not very long ago—the elderly possessed a treasured quality the Japanese call *hinkaku*, variously translated as dignity, elegance, grace, refinement, decorum. The elderly were decorum personified. They cultivated it, nurtured it, served as a model of it for their grandchildren. Grandchildren are a lesser consideration now. If there are any, they're likely to live far away. Increasingly, the elderly live alone—by themselves, for themselves. Their responsibilities in life fulfilled, what remains are entitlements—which, when not acknowledged, must be asserted. The resulting behavior, says the weekly Shukan Post, is plain for all to see, raising the question which headlines its article: "Where has elderly people's hinkaku gone?"

4 "I was on the train home after a long day," recalls a harassed middle-aged company man. "A large group of old people were sitting together. In between two of them was a vacant seat—with a bag on it. 'Is this seat taken?' I asked; 'can I sit down?' 'My friend will be getting on later,' said one of the women, as blasé as you please. Subject closed. What could I do?" Stand and fume.

5 "There was a pregnant lady sitting on a priority seat," says a university student in her teens. "An old woman got on the train. There were no empty seats. So she went up to the pregnant woman: 'I see you're near your time; you'd better stand, or you'll have a difficult delivery.' The pregnant woman demurred: 'It's hard for me to stand.' 'Well then,' said the other, 'you won't have a healthy baby!'" It ended with the pregnant woman standing up, the old woman sitting down, and the student giving up her seat to the pregnant woman.

6 Generally the elderly are portrayed as victims—of infirmity, dementia, fraudsters, uncaring or busy children, bewilderment as social and technological change overwhelms their waning adaptive powers. To Shukan Post, however, they are triumphant conquerors and graceless winners. They have no respect for others' rights or needs. They shout when others want quiet, demand to be served first when others are waiting, adjust hospital air conditioners to suit themselves in defiance of signs asking them not to. A caregiver in her 30s who works at a senior citizens home tells of a man who gropes her while she feeds him. "It's unpleasant," she sighs, "but I put up with it."

7 Most of the evidence is anecdotal, but there's this statistic: In 2013, 23.4 percent of physical attacks on railway personnel were perpetrated by people aged 60 or older.

8 Should the young respect the elderly, pity them, or gnash their teeth at them? Sometimes different generations can seem almost like different species, shaped by environments so different as to almost seem like different planets. Those who came of age amid the postwar ruins, with its grinding poverty and a self-sacrificing work ethic that seems in retrospect vaguely kamikaze-like, pride themselves on having rebuilt Japan; to which those too young to have known anything but the stagnant economy that shadows their almost miraculous technological empowerment might reply, "For whose benefit? Certainly not for ours!" To young adults today, many of them shut out of regular employment and feeling deprived of sufficient financial security to marry, the old are people who coasted through life on the foam of an economic bubble that burst before they could hitch a ride on it; now, say the young, the pension entitlements and medical needs of the old are squeezing the life out of them.

9 It would be interesting to hear what "Masao" (as we'll call him) would reply to that. He'd laugh first of all, for he seems a good-humored old gentleman, despite his adversity—maybe because of it; it seems to amuse him more than it weighs him down. A reporter for Sunday Mainichi magazine found him hard at work at 6 a.m. one morning pushing a heavily-laden cart through a warehouse. He's 80 years old and holds not one job but two, one of the growing ranks of elderly who must work to live because their pensions are inadequate.

10 "I've been doing this since I was young," says Masao, laughing—"40, 50 years. Knees getting a bit tricky, hurt when I walk, but I shift my strength onto the cart and we get along okay. Pension—don't get much 'cause I didn't pay in much. There's nursing care insurance to pay, and… then what? Medical insurance, rent, utilities, food… not much left over after that!" he laughs.

11 Sunday Mainichi's writer visits a Tokyo employment center that reports 28 percent of its job seekers in 2013 were over 65, up from 24 percent in 2012—and yet only 20 percent of senior applicants land jobs. The mismatch between what they want—mostly office jobs that bring their previous experience into play—and what employers who hire seniors want them for—security guards, cleaners—is simply too great.

12 A job for a senior citizen may be a pastime but is at least as likely to be an economic necessity. Pension payments are decreasing—how can they not be? The system was designed, as consultant Keisuke Nakahara tells Shukan Gendai magazine, at a time when people lived an average of 13 years after retirement, mostly with their families; now they might live 30 years and, increasingly, alone. What this can mean is reflected in a statistic cited by Sunday Mainichi: 45.2 percent of social welfare payments are claimed by pensioners at a loss to make ends meet.

13 There are rich elderly and poor elderly, but the bond that unites them—age—may be stronger than any class tensions, just as youth bound rich and poor youngsters together when the world was so incredibly young half a century or so ago. Japan, as everyone knows, is growing older and older. So is the world, but not at Japan's pace. Of the world's roughly 440,000 centenarians, 58,820, as of September, were Japanese.

14 But that's nothing. The weekly magazine Flash quotes researchers who retard the aging process at the cellular level and look ahead to a life expectancy of 300 years. Will we ever grow to love life deeply enough to want to live that long?

cellular：細胞の

(1180 words)

Comprehension Check

1 この記事では高齢者と若者のマナーに関する対立を述べているので、「高齢者」が中心概念です。どのような類義語で言い換えられていますか。

2 高齢者が感じる自負と権利意識について、記事の内容をまとめなさい。

3 若者が年配の人々を敬えない気持ちになるような原因と現状について、この記事で書かれていることをまとめなさい。

Build up Your Vocabulary

1
第5段落に "a pregnant lady"「妊娠した女性」という表現がありますが、これを丁寧に表現すると "an expecting mother" のようになります。これと関連して障害を持つ人を表す丁寧な表現を学びましょう。

目の見えない人
耳の聞こえない人
車椅子に乗っている人

2
第8段落に "regular employment"「正規雇用」、第11段落には "job seekers"「求職者」という表現があります。雇用関係の英語表現を学びましょう。

非正規雇用（不十分雇用）
失業
通勤手当
無断欠勤
扶養手当

3
第13段落に centenarians「百歳代の人」という表現がありますが、70代、80代、90代の人々はどのような英語表現で表しますか。

Helpful Notes

1 ▷ コンマはニュース英語においては特にタイトルやサブタイトルで and の代わりに用いられる。Tokyo, Seoul will talk.「日韓首脳会談が行われる予定」など。

2 ▷ この表現は "She is the epitome of kawaii."「彼女はカワイイという言葉そのもの」"He is what we call a walking dictionary"「彼は物知り」などと比較すべきである。

3 ▷ "Where have all the flowers gone?"「花はどこへ行った」という60年代のヒット曲のタイトル参照。これはさらにラテン語の "Ubi sunt?" = "where are (they)?"「かつてのギリシア・ローマの栄華はどこへいったのか」、良き昔を懐かしむ意の成句にさかのぼる。

4 ▷ 「いたって冷淡に、何の配慮もなく」

5 ▷ 「怒る・腹を立てる」の意には burn, smoke, flare up, boil など「燃える」「煙を出す」「蒸気を出す」「沸騰する」が原義の動詞が転用される。

6 ▷ cf. irregular employment, underemployment, unemployment.

7 ▷ 複数形では「公共事業・企業（電気・ガス・水道会社など）」、転じてここでは「光熱費」。

8 ▷ 動詞 land は「水揚げする＝魚を釣りあげる」の意味から「職を得る」の意味で使われるようになった。同じように狩猟・漁関係の言葉を使った job hunting「職探し」がある。

9 ▷ ここでの動詞 grow は「成長する・年を取る」と「～になる」の意味を掛けてあるらしい。

Current English Composition

次の日本語を英語にしなさい。
ただし、下線を引いた部分は下線部のみを英語にしなさい。

1 年配の人々の間では、日本人の常識が崩れてきているという見方が広まっている。

2 今や65歳以上の運転者の数は1,700万人を上回ると想定され、75歳以上の運転免許保持者は2005年の236万人から昨年には倍に増えて477万人になった。
(第7段落 "aged 60 or older" 参考)

Now the number of drivers aged 65 or older is estimated to be more than 17 million, _____
_____ .

3 一人暮らしの年老いていく人々が増えて、自分の面倒をみることができなくなっていき、老人を蝕む最も恐ろしい病気、認知症に限っても、どのくらいの数の死者が出るかは予想がつく。

More and more older people living alone who are less and less capable of looking after themselves _____
_____ takes its predictable toll.

4 地下鉄の乗客は様々な迷惑行為に不快を感じている。車内で化粧をしたり、酔っぱらって倒れこんだり、携帯電話で大声で話したり、高齢者、体の不自由な人、妊娠している人のための優先座席に座ったり、駆け込み乗車などの行為である。

Subway travelers are embarrassed by such discomfiting activities as _____
_____
_____ or rushing to board as the doors are closing.

Chapter 6
ひきこもりの人を社会へ

日本には大勢のひきこもりの人たちがいます。この現象を引き起こす原因はどこにあるのでしょうか。高齢化社会においてはひきこもりに関しても新たな問題が生じているようです。それは何でしょうか。ひきこもりの人たちを支援するにはどうすれば良いのでしょうか。

III 社会と個人

(左) 研究イベントシンポジウムの様子
(中央) シューレ大学
(右) 平井渚さん
© シューレ大学

Key Words Check

これから読む記事に登場する重要単語をチェックしましょう。
（　）内は該当する段落番号を示しています。

- mobilize (4)
- workforce (4)
- anorexic (6)
- nonprofit (8)
- Cabinet Office (12)
- welfare recipient (16)
- nationwide (17)

Half a million societal drop-outs drag on Abe's economic dreams

1 Nagisa Hirai was an active child who loved playing soccer with the boys. But that early happiness dissipated on her first day at elementary school when she became frightened after being unable to find her classroom.

2 Over time, she became a *hikikomori*, a Japanese term used to describe the more than half a million young people in the country who stay at home and shun interaction with people outside their family. She would suffer anxiety attacks over anything unfamiliar—even forgetting stuff for school could cause her to panic. She became increasingly uncomfortable going to school, pushing her strict parents to force her to attend.

3 The 30-year-old now says she's recovering, but there are still days when she can't drag herself out of bed for her part-time job at a university.

4 While the hikikomori issue isn't new, Prime Minister Shinzo Abe's administration now plans to mobilize them as part of a broader drive to bolster the aging workforce. The prime minister has vowed to stop the population from falling below 100 million from the current 127 million, and have all members of society make an active contribution to the world's third-biggest economy.

5 There is no single cause for the phenomenon. Hikikomori can stem from factors such bullying at school or work, or pressure from parents or other family members to succeed in entrance examinations or job interviews.

6 In Hirai's case, she was both scared of people and felt bad about not being able to go to school. She became anorexic during her time at a part-time high school as she struggled to find a solution—her weight dropping to around 30 kg (66 pounds).

7 "I could suppress my emotions by restraining my appetite," Hirai says. While it allowed her to go out and meet people, she was never able to attend classes and dropped out when her classmates graduated.

8 Hirai received support from Shure University, a nonprofit that provides pressure-free space for people like her that want to continue their education. She's now been living by herself for nearly 10 years and says that although she's getting better she still gets tense around some people.

9 "I'm afraid of shutting myself off again from society," she says of her career plans. "What's more important to me is the kind of people I'm with rather than what I want to do. My parents are already old and I'm only a junior high school graduate. I'm always anxious about how I can live my life."

10 Kageki Asakura, a member of the Shure University, says a lack of self respect is a reason why many people become hikikomori. Negative perceptions toward those who drop out of society make the situation worse, he says.

11 In a government survey published in 2014 of young people in seven countries including Japan, the U.S. and South Korea, Japanese were ranked lowest in terms of self satisfaction. Only 7.5 percent said they were content.

12 About 541,000 people aged between 15 and 39—or 1.6 percent of the population in that age group—were estimated to be hikikomori in a Cabinet Office report published in September. The government defines them as people who have stayed at home and avoided interaction with nonfamily members for at least six months.

13 As society ages, hikikomori are also getting older. About 53 percent of them in Shimane Prefecture were aged 40 or older, with the figure at 44 percent in Yamagata Prefecture. This in turn raises questions about how the older dropouts will support themselves when their aging parents die.

14 Appropriate policies such as financial assistance and counseling could help transform hikikomori into members of the labor force, says Eriko Ito, a consultant at Nomura Research Institute in Tokyo. This would boost overall economic output as well as help reduce spending on social welfare.

15 "We should change our thinking about supporting then," Ito says. "It's an investment, not a cost."

16 Each welfare recipient turned into a taxpayer would add between ¥78 million ($702,000) and ¥98 million to the nation's finances over their lifetime, according to calculations based on the latest available data from the Ministry of Health, Labor and Welfare.

17 The government's plan is to support hikikomori and other young people with difficulties by making them more "independent." It has set up counseling centers nationwide, and has support workers visiting those reluctant to leave home.

18 But reaching out may prove tricky. More than 65 percent of the hikikomori surveyed said they weren't keen on these services as they were concerned about not being able to communicate or reluctant to have other people notice them.

19 "Abe's labor policy is putting pressure on hikikomori," the NPO's Asakura says. "Abe wants them to be great and achieve great results. Why can't they just pursue happiness instead?"

(810 words)

---

labor force：第 4 段落 workforce の言い換え、Chapter 3 参照。

investment：投資

Comprehension Check

1 この記事では「ひきこもり」が中心概念です。ひきこもりの言い換え表現、説明表現を抜き出して、辞書の定義と比較しなさい。

2 第7段落に 平井さんの発言 "I could suppress my emotions by restraining my appetite" が引用されていますが、ここで emotions と複数形になっている理由を考えなさい。

3 平井さんの一番の心配はどのようなことですか。

Build up Your Vocabulary

1
この記事にはCabinet Office 内閣府、Ministry of Health, Labor and Welfare 厚生労働省という省庁名がありました。以下の省庁名、国会関係の組織名を表す英語表現を調べましょう（日本語表記では欠けている部分に注意）。

国土交通省

参議院

通常国会

地方創生担当大臣

文部科学省

2
第4段落に「就労人口、従業員数」を意味するworkforceがあります。これを参考に以下の意味を名詞forceを用いて表してみましょう。

職員から見て、病院の全職員

学生から見て、自分の大学の教授陣

日本人から見た、2020年東京オリンピックの日本人選手団

特別調査団（←特認部隊）

3
第6段落にanorexic「拒食症の」という形容詞があります。これに関連して以下の意味の英語表現を学習しましょう。

摂食障害

過食症

発達障害

学習困難児童

自閉症

ゲーム障害

4
第8段落にpressure-free spaceという表現があります。この形を参考に以下の意味を英語で表してみましょう。

免税店

禁煙社会

核兵器のない世界

歩行者天国（の街路）

Helpful Notes

1 ▷ 「ひきこもり」は日本の社会現象として国際的な認知と注目を受けて、*The Oxford English Dictionary* の見出し語としても既に採録され、イタリアでもひきこもりと見られる人が推定10万人ほどいるとされ、社会心理学者が立ち上げた Hikikomori Italia というウェブサイトもできた。

2 ▷ 動詞 mobilize は「（国民を兵士として）動員する」が原義である。この文中の workforce は就労人口、従業員を軍隊に見立てた表現であるから、この mobilize が巧く組合わさっている。

3 ▷ シューレ大学。東京都新宿区にある非営利組織で、学生が運営に関わって行事や講義の内容を決めていく形をとっている。

Current English Composition

次の日本語を英語にしなさい。
ただし、下線を引いた部分は下線部のみを英語にしなさい。

1 ひきこもりになった人は、<u>外部の世界とコミュニケーションをとるのがとても難しいと感じている</u>。

Socially withdrawn people _____

_____ .

2 自国でのひきこもりの増加に対応するために、<u>イタリアの若い社会心理学者が「ひきこもりイタリア」というウェブサイトを立ち上げた</u>。

_____

_____ to respond to the increase of

hikikomori in the country.

3 厚生労働省の調査で顕著になった最近の傾向は、<u>独身のままでいる事を選ぶ人が増えたことだ</u>。

According to a survey by the Ministry of Health and Welfare, a tendency in

recent years _____

_____ .

4 日本の高齢者の人口が増える一方で、平均的な家族のサイズが縮まってきた。水曜日に発表された国勢調査の結果で、<u>65歳以上の高齢者は全人口の26.7%を占めることがわかった</u>。(13段落の "aged 40 or older" 参考)

The number of elderly people in Japan has increased, while the average family

has shrunk in size. _____

_____ , census data released Wednesday reveal.

Chapter 7

いじめと教師の過労

「ブラック企業」と呼ばれる職場の存在が世間の注目を集めていますが、学校までもがブラック職場と化しているという指摘があります。学校の先生たちはどのような苦しみを味わっているのでしょうか。彼らの疲弊は教育現場にどのような影響を与えているのでしょうか。

Key Words Check

これから読む記事に登場する重要単語をチェックしましょう。
（　）内は該当する段落番号を示しています。

- compulsive (1)
- side effect (2)
- obnoxious (3)
- impervious (5)
- cauldron (8)
- emeritus (11)
- flux (13)

The education system still has much to learn

1 There is a driven, compulsive quality to Japanese education, which emerges clearly in a report by Shukan Toyo Keizai magazine titled "Schools are breaking down."

2 Technological progress has a side-effect: an economy that demands higher and higher education as the price of admission into it. Children struggle to learn, and teachers to teach, more and more. Two resulting symptoms are overworked teachers and bullied, or bullying, children.

3 *Karōshi* (death from overwork) is a familiar phenomenon in the private sector but not one commonly associated with the teaching profession. And yet 60 percent of public junior high school teachers are "borderline karōshi," Toyo Keizai says, meaning they work at least 60 hours a week, though contracted to work only 38 hours, 45 minutes. The overtime hours, largely unpaid, are spent preparing lessons, grading assignments and tests, supervising extra-curricular activities, counseling, dealing with concerned and/or obnoxious parents, attending meetings, handling administrative chores and so on.

4 One teacher, in November 2011, actually did work himself to death. He was 26 and in his second year of teaching junior high school in Osaka. He was dedicated. He thought his students deserved everything he had to give, and he gave everything. He collapsed one day in his apartment. He'd suffered a stroke. It took three years for his death to be officially recognized as karōshi.

5 Bullying is an old story, hardly confined to Japan, seemingly impervious to decades' worth of measures to reduce it. In fact it's rising. In extreme forms it amounts to nothing less than torture, physical and psychological. The ubiquitous smartphone makes the latter easy. You can say anything you like about anyone you don't like. Smearing a classmate all over the net is an easy way to vent stress you can't cope with otherwise —partly caused, maybe, by classmates smearing *you* all over the net.

6 In 2015, there were roughly 220,000 officially recognized bullying episodes in elementary, junior high and senior high schools nationwide —the most ever, nearly double the figure for 2006. Part of the increase is due to stricter reporting requirements. Schools were too apt to turn a blind eye. They had reputations to protect. A notorious instance, the immediate cause of the heightened requirements, was the suicide in 2011 of a boy in Otsu, Shiga Prefecture. It took the school two years to admit the boy had been bullied. Over 300 children a year in Japan kill themselves—320 in 2016. The overall suicide rate is declining, but not the under-18 suicide rate, unchanged over the past decade. School can make childhood a living hell, unknown and unknowable to adults.

7 Toyo Keizai fears schools are going "black." The reference is to *burakku kigyō* (black companies) that overwork and underpay employees to the point of neo-slavery. In the private sector, one-third of the workforce is officially part time—which is to say, paid like part-timers, though often worked like full-timers. Public elementary junior and senior high schools seem to be moving in that direction. As of 2013, one-sixth of their teaching staffs nationwide were part time. It saves money. A 41-year-old part-time teacher in her seventh year earns ¥2.46 million a year—roughly a third of a veteran full-time teacher's salary, and little enough, ironically, to make her eligible for limited welfare assistance. Adding insult to injury, she never knows from one year to the next whether her contract will be renewed.

8 What, one wonders, of the quality of education in such a cauldron as the public education system seems to be, if Toyo Keizai's picture is anything to go by? Much is made of international rankings, specifically those of the OECD's Program for International Student Assessment (PISA), and Japan doesn't fare too badly: second among OECD advanced nations in "science literacy" in 2015, up from fourth in 2012; fifth in "mathematical literacy," up from seventh. The weak link in the chain is *literacy* literacy—more literally, reading comprehension—in which Japan ranked eighth, down from fourth.

9 Maybe science and mathematics are enough. Who needs words when you have numbers? This or that individual, or this or that employer, might not, but civilization as a whole might. The education ministry seems to think it does. Its introduction of moral education as a formal subject, effective next April, suggests as much.

10 An episode that occurred in Okinawa last month will bolster the view that a moral vacuum exists, which moral education must fill. Four teenagers allegedly vandalized a memorial in a cave in which civilians were forced to commit mass suicide in the closing days of World War II.

11 Teens do crazy things; it's part of growing up, and maybe too much shouldn't be made of it. But this particular stunt suggests a blindness and deafness to tragedy that Okinawa International University professor emeritus Masaie Ishihara, for one, sees as an education problem.

12 "I suspect," Ishihara told the Mainichi Shimbun, "that history, and what happened during the Battle of Okinawa, are not being passed down to younger generations in education."

13 It's hard to "pass down" the past to a present in such rapid flux. Toyo Keizai mentions yet another burden on educators. Traditionally, school was one of three "pillars" in a child's education. The other two were family and community. Career-oriented parents and weakened community ties leave school shouldering a near-monopoly that would strain it even under ideal circumstances, which present ones are not. Schools have their hands full keeping kids technologically primed. Kindergartens are teaching computer programming. The past? Who needs it? Who has time for it?

14 "Who needs it?" is a good question. There's the all-too-oft-quoted line about those who forget the past being doomed to repeat it. If George Santayana, whose line it is, meant war, his thinking is open to question. Historical memory, and the resentments it breeds, have caused at least as many wars as historical forgetfulness. North Korea seethes not because it has forgotten the Japanese occupation but because it remembers it.

15 What to teach, how and to whom are permanent questions, increasingly urgent as postmodern civilization careens into an unknown future. If Toyo Keizai is right about schools "breaking down," it's a bad time for it to be happening.

(1048 words)

Comprehension Check

1 現代の学校ではいじめの件数が増加しているということが本文で述べられていますが、いじめの質とその原因についてはどのように説明されていますか。

2 第 10 段落に見られる "moral vacuum" とはどのような内容か、本文に示された具体例を用いて説明しなさい。

3 この記事の末尾は "If Toyo Keizai is right about schools "breaking down," it's a bad time for it to be happening." という文で結ばれていますが、なぜ "a bad time" と言えるのでしょうか。本文の内容に即して説明しなさい。

Build up Your Vocabulary

1
この記事では "nearly double the figure for 2006"（第6段落）、"one-sixth of their teaching staffs nationwide" のような倍数・分数表記が出てきました。以下の分数・倍数を英語ではどのように表現するか確認しましょう。

1/2　　　　　　　3倍の数
2/3　　　　　　　4倍の大きさ
1/4
15/37

2
第10段落で World War II「第二次世界大戦」という言葉が出てきますが、the second world war/the Second World War という言い方もあります。数字を含む以下の日本語を2種の英語表現で表しましょう。

21世紀

本の第3章

新幹線の5号車

3
第13段落に "yet another burden"「さらにまた別の重荷（が教師たちに加わる）」という表現があります。同種の現象や事柄を繰り返した後で、さらにもう一つ言及する際に用いられます。同じく、何かを比較をした後でさらに上のものを出す時に、この yet や still, even という副詞が用いられます。以下の日本語を英語で表してみましょう。

フェイクニュースについての更なる問題

もっと良い解決方法

またもや出た新しい発明品

4
第2段落に side effect「副作用、副産物」という語があります。副作用、副産物を意味する類語を調べて覚えましょう。

Helpful Notes

1 ▷『週刊東洋経済』2017年9月16日号では「学校が壊れる：学校は完全なブラック職場だ」という特集が組まれ、学校教員が過重労働を強いられている実態に焦点が当てられている。
2 ▷ 2011年、大阪府の堺市立深井中学校の理科教諭、前田大仁（ひろひと）氏（当時26歳）が過労の末、出勤前に倒れて死亡した。
3 ▷ 日本語の「泣きっ面に蜂」、「踏んだり蹴ったり」などに近い意味の英語の定型句で、<in-> の頭韻句となっている。
4 ▷ 第二次大戦末期（1945年）の沖縄戦で住民が集団自決（強制集団死）に追い込まれた沖縄県読谷村（よみたんそん）の自然壕「チビチリガマ」の内部の遺骨や遺品が壊されているのが2017年9月12日に発覚。3日後、地元の16～19歳の4人が器物損壊容疑で逮捕された。
5 ▷ 第8段落の "much is made of" と同じく "make much/ little of ~"「～を重視する／軽視する」という定型表現の受動態てあること注意。
6 ▷ この表現では、建物を支える柱を組織や主義主張における重要要素、不可欠要素を意味する比喩として、後続文中の shouldering「責任を担う」と呼応させて用いている。それがなくなると崩れてしまう、という含意。Four pillars of democracy「民主主義の4本の柱」、three pillars of the United Nations「国際連合の3本の柱」のように使う。
7 ▷ ジョージ・サンタヤナ（1863-1952）はスペイン生まれのアメリカの哲学者・詩人。

Current English Composition

次の日本語を英語にしなさい。
ただし、下線を引いた部分は下線部のみを英語にしなさい。

1 過労死とは、仕事のし過ぎや仕事に関連した消耗によって引き起こされ、その犠牲者は、かつては典型的に 40 代、50 代の中間管理職であった。（第 3 段落関連）

The victims of karoshi, or death brought on by overwork or job-related exhaustion, _____
_____ .

2 このほど初めて過労死の現状を報告する政府の白書が出たが、問題はここに示されたデータをどのように受けとり、どういう対策をとるかである。
（第 8 段落、第 11 段落 "much is made of" 参考）

As the nation's first white paper on "karoshi" was released and the situation was detailed, _____
_____ .

3 最近では、先生が個人で生徒一人一人の要求に対応するのがますます難しくなってきた。

It is growing ever more difficult _____
_____ .

4 中学校でのいじめは、たぶん若者が経験する最も激しい苦難であろう。なぜなら、たいていの子供は、社会のルールがまだ若い自分たちには適用されないと思っているからだ。

_____
_____ . Most kids are still at the age where they do not feel the rules of society apply to them.

Chapter 8

ブラックバイト

はたらけどはたらけど猶（なお）わがくらし楽にならざり…明治時代の石川啄木の声が、新たな響きで私たちに迫ります。若者を搾取する新たな労働形態、ブラックバイトとはいかなるものなのでしょうか。

IV 雇用と労働

© Fast&Slow / PIXTA

© ocsa / PIXTA

Key Words Check

これから読む記事に登場する重要単語をチェックしましょう。
（　）内は該当する段落番号を示しています。

- neologism (2)
- extrapolate (2)
- quota (6)
- workplace abuse (7)
- allegedly (11)
- outspoken (12)
- harangue (13)
- dispensation (14)

A dark force targets youth at their jobs

1 In the ongoing discussion about workplace abuse, the media has advanced yet another new term. "Black *baito*" modifies the already popular phrase "black *kigyō*," which are companies that manipulate or ignore labor standards in order to get employees to work overtime without pay. "Baito" is an abbreviation of *arbeit*, the German word that in Japan stands for part-time work, so "black baito" refers specifically to part-time workers.

2 A recent feature in the Tokyo Shimbun described the issue in detail using as examples young people who attend Tokyo's Waseda University. One, a male senior, works for a "major clothing chain" where "overtime is prohibited." He explains that if an employee works more hours than his shift designates, he has to submit a *shimatsusho* (written apology), but it's usually "impossible" to complete assignments within his work shift, so he goes back to work for no pay after punching out. This is called "service baito," a neologism extrapolated from the term "service *zangyō*" (unpaid overtime).

3 A female junior who works for a "major coffee shop chain" testifies that every day she works at least "an extra 15 minutes" without pay after her store closes for the day, and often as much as 45 minutes. She's never paid for this time. A female senior who teaches at a cram school is compelled to meet with students out of class to discuss "summer seminars" in an effort to get them to sign up for them. She is not compensated for these meetings.

4 A male junior who works for a "well-known hamburger chain" describes working all night without pay to clean the restaurant prior to an inspection by the head office.

5 The list goes on and includes other universities and other types of businesses. Hirokazu Ouchi, the Chukyo University professor who coined the term "black baito," tells the paper that these companies "know these employees are students working part-time, but they don't respect the fact that they have to study."

6 One way of getting them to work more is to impose quotas. A Teikyo University sophomore who works for a "big *gyūdon* (beef bowl) chain" says he has to sell a minimum number of dishes during a given shift. If he doesn't, then he feels he has to remain at work until he does, and isn't paid for the extra time. "Students who are subjected to black baito think it's natural," Ouchi says. "They have no understanding of their rights as workers."

7 The professor is now working with lawyers to promote greater knowledge of labor standards among part-timers, who are overlooked in the debate about workplace abuse. Students are especially vulnerable because they tend to be financially disadvantaged. According to the National Federation of University Cooperative Associations, university students on average received ¥102,240 a month from their parents in 1996. This amount dropped to ¥72,280 by 2013. In 1996, 2.2 percent of students received no money from their parents. Now, it's 8.8 percent. Meanwhile,

punch out：タイムカードに打刻して退社する

compel：強いる

vulnerable：立場が弱い

tuition has increased and terms for student loans are becoming stricter, so more students have to work their way through college.

8 However, Ouchi mentions several companies that have improved workplace conditions for part-timers, specifically the fast food chain Sukiya, which has discontinued its practice of staffing outlets with one employee late at night, and discount clothing giant Uniqlo, which now posts its salary schedules. Ouchi says these two companies did this because "society started paying attention," and the reason society paid attention is that the media named these companies in their coverage of workplace abuse.

9 As is often pointed out in this column, the press tends to avoid naming names when it comes to consumer or work-related issues that might reflect badly on private firms. The above-mentioned victims of workplace abuse still toil for their problem companies, and exposing the names of those companies may put them at risk of losing their jobs. Another less justifiable explanation is that most media still rely on advertising and thus don't want to upset a current or potential revenue source.

10 In the case of Uniqlo, a business magazine first reported on the retail chain's workplace abuse, thus providing an excuse for the rest of the media to follow suit. Sukiya was being investigated by the authorities. As already existing "news" their abuses could then be reported by the mass media openly.

11 The successful Watami restaurant chain was the poster boy for black kigyō for a number of years, mainly because one of its employees committed suicide, allegedly due to overwork. But another reason is that the president of Watami, Miki Watanabe, is a high-profile media figure.

12 Another such figure is Yuri Takano, the founder of Fuji Beauty, a popular "aesthetic" salon specializing in weight loss and hair removal. As explained in the magazine Cyzo, Takano regularly appears on television as a guest because she can save money on advertising. She is outspoken, so producers like to hire her, and every time she shows up on the air she boosts her brand for free. In fact, she gets paid for it.

13 However, by doing so, Takano exposes herself to scrutiny, especially since she likes to brag about her wealth (three vacation homes, including one in Hawaii), and the media has been quick to report on her company's labor violations and how her extravagance can be traced to profits based on black kigyō practices. In August, Nihon Keizai Shimbun reported that Takano blasted a group of employees at her Sendai branch for complaining to the Labor Standards Bureau about the imposition of quotas and warned that if they joined a union, "this company will go bankrupt." Her harangue lasted two hours. She is now being investigated.

14 Takano is "paying the fame tax," in Cyzo's words. By taking advantage of TV's desire for outsized personalities she loses the dispensation that paid advertisers enjoy with relation to the media. But more importantly, when you dare to be notorious, you're fair game.

(1010 words)

Comprehension Check

1 この記事では「ブラックバイト」について実例を挙げて論じていますが、「ブラックバイト」という労働形態はどのようなものなのか、またなぜそのような形態が成立するのかを簡潔に説明しなさい。

2 過去と現在の大学生の財政事情について、まとめなさい。

3 第9段落で、"As is often pointed out in this column, the press tends to avoid naming names when it comes to consumer or work-related issues that might reflect badly on private firms." と述べられていますが、なぜそのような傾向が生じるのか、その理由を述べなさい。また、この現象は本記事自体にも見られます。その箇所を指摘しなさい。

Build up Your Vocabulary

1

この記事に出てくる大学生の学年を表す表現を抜き出しなさい。

2

第7段落の表現 "terms for student loans" における名詞 term の意味は条件です。この多義語の意味を辞書で確認し、以下の日本語に相当する英語表現を書いてみましょう。

（大学の）春学期

法律用語

大統領の任期は4年です

私は彼と仲が良い

3

第12段落に outspoken「思ったことを口に出す、歯に衣を着せぬ」という形容詞があります。これと関連して、「物言いが柔らかな」「口数の多い、おしゃべりな」など、発言に関わる態度を表す形容詞を調べましょう。

4

第13段落に "Sendai branch"「仙台支社」と言う表現があります。会社関係の以下の語句に相当する英語表現を学びましょう。

本社

子会社

（企業の）吸収合併

企業買収

業務提携

経営破綻

Helpful Notes

1 ▷ "Toyo Keizai mentions yet another burden on educators" Chapter 7 第13段落参照。
2 ▷ ここの内容に興味がある人は『週刊文春』の2016年12月の数週連続記事とThe Japan Times "Undercover journalist infiltrates Uniqlo" (2016年12月18日号、p. 19) を参照。
3 ▷ この段落の文章は第12段落最終文 "she gets paid" を受けて、動詞 pay を中心に皮肉な内容を強調していること注意。成句 "fair game" は「（禁猟期が明けて）狩猟対象となる獣鳥」の意。つまり「攻撃してもかまわない」。しかし「フェアな試合＝従業員を酷使せずきちんと待遇する」の裏意をほのめかせているか。

Current English Composition

次の日本語を英語にしなさい。
ただし、下線を引いた部分は下線部のみを英語にしなさい。

1 今朝の電車は満員だった。**私は肘で他の乗客をかき分けて出た。**（第 7 段落 "work their way through college"「自分で働いて学費を稼ぎ、大学を卒業する」参考）

This morning my train was jam-packed. _____
_____ .

2 たいていの店舗ではパートタイムのスタッフは大学生で、**正社員も 20 代 30 代の若い人たちである。**（第 8 段落 outlets 参考）

At most outlets, the part-time staff is made up of college students, _____
_____ .

3 日本は、2015 年に北部太平洋のクロマグロ幼魚の漁獲量を半分に減らす計画で、**他の国々がこれにならうことを望んでいる。**（第 10 段落 follow suit 参考）

Japan plans to slash by half the amount of juvenile bluefin tuna taken from the Northern Pacific starting in 2015 _____
_____ .

4 女性を経済活動にもっと参入させよと強く主張する人もいるが、**調査してみると、そうすることで国内総生産がかなり増える計算となる。**（第 13 段落 by doing so 参考）

There's a powerful argument for more women in the economy _____
_____
_____ .

Chapter 9

24時間7日労働

働く日本人を取り巻く環境は、決して良いとは言えません。政府や財界のてこ入れにもかかわらず、労働環境がなかなか改善されないのはなぜでしょうか。苛烈な労働は人間の心身にどのような影響を与えるのでしょうか。

IV 雇用と労働

Key Words Check

これから読む記事に登場する重要単語をチェックしましょう。
（ ）内は該当する段落番号を示しています。

- hyper-competitive (2)
- extinct (2)
- depression (3)
- punch line (5)
- exploitation (6)
- compliance (8)
- ceiling (11)
- resilient (12)
- innuendo (14)

The unbearable burden of 24/7 work

1 There was no nonsense about the 1990s in Japan. The economy had crashed, the bubble had burst. "The age of human relationships is over," declared a corporate executive to Aera magazine in 1996, defending the cost-cutting layoffs then gathering speed. "This is the era of the discount store. The only sales criterion is: How cheaply are you selling?"

2 No nonsense then, no nonsense now. We're in the same era—a different, more mature phase of it, maybe. Twenty years ago the issue was layoffs. Now it's overwork. They are two faces of the same coin: cost-cutting. A hyper-competitive economy demands ruthlessness. Human relationships? Now as then: not extinct, but struggling.

3 Mass layoffs followed by a prolonged hiring freeze sum up a significant chunk of the economic history of the past two decades. Hiring has revived lately, unemployment is low, most workers are working—but at what? What kind of a life is your job giving you? Sometimes it gives you death; 93 cases of *karōshi* (death from overwork) have been officially recognized in Japan in fiscal 2015. They are extreme cases. Generally you don't die from work. Stress, depression and chronic fatigue are not necessarily fatal.

4 "No matter how much I rest, I'm always tired," a company employee in his 40s complains to Spa! magazine. Weekly Playboy magazine, polling 1,000 workers, found 59 percent of the 878 who routinely worked overtime were staggering "somewhat" if not "very much" under the burden of their jobs.

5 There's a cute commercial jingle from the '80s, considered very effective in its time, that would sound like mockery today—a measure of the sea change we've been through. It advertised an energy drink. While a young executive gulping it down fairly bursts with vigor and vitality, a spirited masculine voice belts out the punch line: "Can you fight 24 hours a day, businessman?" The expression on the executive's face suggests 24 hours are hardly enough for him.

6 The term "*burakku kigyō*" ("black company") was unknown in those halcyon days when work was life and not, as it often is now, life-threatening or life-degrading. "Black company" has no formal definition, but what it conveys is a degree of exploitation bordering on slavery. A recent survey by the Japanese Trade Union Confederation (Rengo) found one-quarter of 2,000 respondents—and one-third of men in their 20s and 30s—feel they work for black companies.

7 A black-company employee has this advantage over a slave: freedom to quit. Weekly Playboy introduces "A-san," in whose case that freedom seems purely nominal. He's 28 and works as an assembly line supervisor for a mid-size Tohoku food processing firm. His salary is roughly ¥200,000 a month. His work hours are 8 a.m. to 4:30 p.m., meaning that's what he gets paid for, though in fact he's on the job from 6:30 a.m. to 6 p.m., when business is relatively slow.

8 When it's rushed, from July through November, 140 overtime hours a month are normal. Under governmental and economic pressure,

ruthlessness：無慈悲

chronic：Chapter 11 第7段落 chronic manpower shortage 参照。

jingle：コマーシャル・ソング

slavery：Chapter 7 第7段落 neo slavery 参照。

nominal：有名無実の

companies are scrambling to reduce overtime. A-san's employer is no exception. When labor bureau inspectors came by and demanded overtime be limited to 42 hours a month, the company promptly went into compliance mode. A-san laughs sardonically. "The only change," he says, "is that now I only get paid for 42 hours. The workload is still the same."

9 So why doesn't he quit? He would, if he could find a better job. So far he hasn't been able to. He's supposed to be getting married soon but wonders if it's possible under the present circumstances. "Human relationships" may have to wait.

10 Weekly Playboy's coverage treats us to the somewhat absurd spectacle of employees sneaking in to their work stations at all hours, against company efforts to get them in and out within regulation time. The trouble with regulation time is that workloads are too much for it. If you don't work overtime—paid or unpaid—you get blamed for not doing your job.

11 That's the plight "Mr. B" finds himself in. He's a 36-year-old restaurant manager employed by a chain of family restaurants. The head office—again, under labor bureau pressure—has imposed a 60-hour ceiling on monthly overtime, and checks computerized clocking-in to make sure employees observe it. Same rock, same hard place: You want to get out as badly as your employer wants to get you out, but only a reduced workload can make reduced working hours realistic, and that reduced workload is not forthcoming, so B-san routinely starts his day two hours before clocking in and finishes it two hours after.

12 It gets worse as you get older, says Spa! Playboy's targeted readership is younger than Spa!'s, whose subjects are in their 40s. It's a tough age. Experience has multiplied your responsibilities, which seems fitting, but body and brain are starting to show their age, growing ever so slightly less resilient than they used to be, to say nothing of the onslaught of domestic worries like financing the kids' college education and seeing parents through their early stages of elderly infirmity. It's enough to keep anyone awake nights.

13 Wakeful nights are a big part of the story. In your 40s especially, says Spa!, sleep quality deteriorates. You're just about to drift off when thoughts invade the brain and get it churning: the mistake you made today, the presentation you must make tomorrow, the blundering or insolent subordinate you'll have to deal with somehow, sometime. Has a client sent an email? Should you check? The 24/7 life is pervasive, and hard to turn off. A drink seems called for—a soothing, calming drink. Wrong, say the experts. Drinking at bedtime is the worst thing you can do. You'll sleep, but not well. What, then? Best, says a clinician the magazine speaks to, is to talk your worries over with someone. Friend? Loved one? Human relationships again. If you have any.

14 Matsuri Takahashi has been much in the news lately, nearly a year after her death. She was a 24-year-old freshman employee of the

plight：苦しい状態

onslaught：猛攻、殺到

blundering：ヘマな、ミスをおかした

advertising giant Dentsu whose suicide last Christmas Day was officially recognized in September as karōshi. Shukan Bunshun magazine described her working life as an endless round of 12-hour days seasoned with insults and innuendoes from superiors persistent enough to qualify as power harassment. Hours before her death, the magazine says, she emailed her mother: "Work is unbearable. Life is unbearable." Would a friend have helped Takahashi? Maybe—if she'd had time for friendship.

(1100 words)

Comprehension Check

1 第8段落では "Under governmental and economic pressure, companies are scrambling to reduce overtime." と述べられていますが、企業は具体的にどのような取り組みを見せているか、そしてその取り組みは功を奏しているか否か、説明しなさい。

2 第12段落冒頭に "It gets worse as you get older, ..." とありますが、年齢が高くなるにつれて浮上する新たな問題はどのようなものですか。まとめなさい。

3 記事最後の高橋さんについての言及の意味するところを、先行する記事の内容と絡めて考えなさい。

Build up Your Vocabulary

1

第2段落に hyper-competitive という言葉が出てきます。接頭辞 hyper- を持つ最近よく使われる英語表現を調べましょう。

超高齢社会（今の日本のこと）

超インフレ

注意欠陥多動性障害

ハイパーメディア

超音速

2

第2段落の終わりに形容詞 extinct「絶滅した」が出てきます。これと関連して、温暖化・環境破壊による種の生存の危険を意味する一連の表現を調べましょう。

3

第11段落に「上限」という意味の名詞 ceiling が出てきました。同じように家屋の部分を表す名詞がどのような比喩的意味で使われるか調べましょう。

threshold
door
window
wall
roof
pillar

Helpful Notes

1 ▷ no-nonsense「馬鹿げたことを許さない、真面目な」「経済的な、効率的な」「簡素な、質素な」
2 ▷ シェイクスピアの戯曲 *Tempest* (l. ii. 400)『あらし』に由来する表現で、世の中の大きな変化について用いる語。
3 ▷ 1989年〜俳優の時任三郎が出演していた第一三共ヘルスケアの栄養ドリンク「リゲイン」のコマーシャル。
4 ▷ 文字通りには「カワセミが現れる日」。海が凪いだ穏やかな日のことで、バブルとその崩壊後の経済の混乱状態にある現在、温暖化の進む異常気象が多い昨今、昔を懐かしんで使われる言葉。
5 ▷ 仕事の閑散期。反義語は次に出る rushed 繁忙期。
6 ▷ 早朝や深夜などの変な時に、尋常ではない時間帯に。Cf. odd hours
7 ▷ ここの badly は「悪く」ではなく very much「大いに」の意味であること注意。
8 ▷ 電通においては1991年に入社2年目の男性社員（当時24歳）が過労自殺しており、その男性の家族が起こした訴訟は2000年に最高裁で会社側の責任が認定され、会社が遺族に賠償金を支払うことで和解が成立した。2013年には男性社員（当時30歳）が病死、その後、過労死と認定された。2017年9月、電通社長が高橋さんの死について正式謝罪を行なった。

Current English Composition

次の日本語を英語にしなさい。
ただし、下線を引いた部分は下線部のみを英語にしなさい。

1 日本には死に至る心臓病に苦しむ子供がたくさんいます。<u>彼らは命を救うことができる移植手術を待っています。</u>
（第 6 段落 "life-threatening or life-degrading." 参考）

There are many children with life-threatening heart's deterioration; _____
_____ .

2 結婚する人が減り、出生率も下がり、人口も高齢化する中で、<u>生涯の最後を一人で迎えることになる高齢者がますます増えている</u>。
（第 11 段落 "That's the plight "Mr. B" finds himself in." 参照）

With the marriage rate slumping, along with the birth rate, and the population ageing rapidly, _____
_____ .

3 新興国の市場は、最近景気後退の兆候を示しだした。
（第 12 段落 "body and brain are starting to show their age" 参照）

4 最近の日本人には、睡眠をきちんと取れない人が多い。
▶これを異なる構文の英文で書いてみましょう（第 13 段落参照）。

Chapter 10

生涯雇用の消失

IV 雇用と労働

大学を卒業して経営の安定した企業に入れば定年まで安泰、そのような気楽な時代は終わりを告げました。終身雇用制度の崩壊に伴い、この制度を支える柱であった年功序列制度も揺れています。

Key Words Check

これから読む記事に登場する重要単語をチェックしましょう。
（　）内は該当する段落番号を示しています。

- in-house (1)
- engender (2)
- storied (3)
- cohort (4)
- drag (4)
- cliche (6)
- lobby (7)
- monolithic (8)
- zero-sum (9)

Debating the merits of lifetime employment

1 Some years ago I worked for a language-teaching service that offered in-house classes for companies. One client was a major electronics manufacturer, and many of the students were trained engineers assigned to the sales division.

2 This human resources tactic always struck me as counter-productive, since those men (always men) possessed practical technical know-how that seemed to be wasted on *eigyō* (sales), but the longer I worked with them the more I grasped the logic, even if I never bought it. Rotating employees throughout the company by means of regular interdepartmental transfers engendered loyalty because they came to understand the workings of the organization, and not just the part they were ostensibly hired to serve.

3 Recently, I came across an explication of this practice in an article in the business magazine Diamond about *nenkō joretsu*, the seniority wage system that is central to Japan's storied lifetime-employment system. The magazine said that interdepartmental transfers provided employees with "experience," but only within a single company, because, in accordance with lifetime employment, employees were hired straight from university and expected to remain with the company until they retired. In other economies, "experience" is the measure by which a prospective employee is evaluated, and the wider and more varied that experience, the more money he or she can theoretically demand. In Japan, it's the opposite. When you leave a company and join another, regardless of your skills, you start back at the bottom of the salary pyramid, because in accordance with the seniority wage system your worth is pegged to how many years you have worked for the *same employer*.

4 Japanese companies have been chipping away at lifetime employment for 20 years now, because it doesn't make sense in an economy that no longer grows as fast as it once did. Diamond says only 8.8 percent of Japanese companies have retained lifetime employment. However, the seniority wage system is still in force because older workers were hired with such expectations, and since salaries under this system are not determined by achievement or even promotion, but rather by how long the individual has been with the organization, there are a lot of *hatarakanai ojisan* (middle-aged men who don't work) on payrolls. The Ministry of Internal Affairs estimates that there are presently 25 million company workers in Japan who fall within the late-40s to mid-60s age cohort, and since productivity peaks around 45, these workers represent a drag on profitability, the implication being that the seniority wage system is a negative incentive. Older workers just cruise to the finish line.

5 Diamond doesn't offer an opinion on this phenomenon. If anything, the magazine plays it for laughs with a rundown of the "Seven types of hatarakanai ojisan," including workers who "delegate everything," who pointlessly criticize subordinates out of habit, who still rely on "skills that are no longer relevant in today's business environment" and, most

ostensibly：名目上

economies：(ひとつの経済圏としての)国。複数形に注意。

chip away at：削って行く

fall within：分類される

delegate：職務を委任する、自分でやらない

significantly, who "sigh a lot" while despairing that things "used to be better."

6 TV scriptwriters and manga artists have exploited these cliches for years, but the impact of seniority on the Japanese economy is being taken seriously by the government. Prime Minister Shinzo Abe has asked a study group in the labor ministry to look at the system with an eye toward having it replaced with a merit-pay system. The thinking is that as long as companies are pledged to offer unproductive older workers more money as they age, there is less money to pay younger employees who need it to make homes and raise families.

7 At least two newspapers have criticized the plan. In an editorial, Tokyo Shimbun blasted the administration for siding with corporate management in its desire to maximize profits by restructuring salaries, and drew a straight line from Abe's proposal to the recent announcement by the Japan Business Federation (Keidanren) that it would resume contributions to political parties. The newspaper argues that "suddenly" changing the system may mean thousands of middle-aged workers will be cut adrift and left unemployable, since the current system hasn't prepared them for a merit-based job market. And changing the system will not necessarily help younger workers, to whom salary scales may not apply because increasingly they tend to be nonregular employees. Moreover, the discussion is being led by the government and the business lobby, with no input from the labor side. The government should just let labor and management work it out on a company-by-company basis.

8 If the editorial has a pandering tone, that could be due to the fact that only older people still read newspapers. A more nuanced criticism was offered by financial editor Yuichi Kojin in the Asahi Shimbun, who acknowledges that the seniority system leads to de facto "psychological retirement" by the time a regular employee reaches their late 40s, because if they haven't been promoted by then they won't see any point in applying themselves anymore. However, Kojin's own research found that the seniority system isn't as monolithic as people think it is. Many companies find ways of either pushing nonproductive workers out or reducing their pay. Rather than doing away with seniority altogether, he thinks it should be altered so that pay is determined by the position, as is usually the case in other countries, and not by the person. That way, older workers understand their situations better, and younger workers can plan for their futures.

9 What bothers Kojin isn't so much doing away with wage seniority, but rather the government's acceptance of the Keidanren assertion that pay is a zero-sum game: You take away money from one group of workers and pay it to another group of workers based on notions of "potential" benefit to the company. The idea that all the workers might share in the success of that company doesn't seem to enter into the equation.

(997 words)

pandering：(年配社員に) 迎合する、おもねる

apply oneself：精力を注ぐ

Comprehension Check

1 この記事の筆者は技術者を営業部に配属させるような日本企業の人材活用戦術について、どのように認識していましたか。またその認識はやがてどのように変化しましたか。

2 日本政府は年功序列制について検討を始めようとしていますが、それはどのような検討で、どのような考え方に基づくものですか。それぞれをまとめなさい。

3 年功序列制の問題点、および年功序列制を廃止することの問題点について、この記事ではさまざまな意見が紹介されています。それぞれをまとめなさい。

Build up Your Vocabulary

1

第1段落に sales division「営業部門」という表現があります。これと関連して、会社の部局を意味する英語表現を学習しましょう。

人事課

研究開発部

財務・経理

広報課

総務部

2

第8段落に "only older people still read newspapers." という文がありますが、この比較級 older はここでは社員を若手 (younger) と年配におおよそ二分しています。比較級と原級を含む次の2組 (a-b, c-d) の英文の相違をよく考えましょう。

a) The prime minister, who **earlier this year** sought a constitutional amendment by 2020, has indicated that he would seek to deepen discussions on the issue to build a broad consensus on an amendment within both the ruling and opposition parties.

b) Oil prices jumped on recent news that OPEC and non-OPEC members agreed to a modest cut in crude oil output that are to gradually take effect in **early this year**.

c) The government is considering dropping its plan to set and announce in September the dates of Emperor Akihito's abdication and the start of a new era, sources said. A decision on the schedule is likely to be postponed until **later this year**.

d) He can delay a decision on whether to now seek a bilateral trade deal until after an election that could come **late this year** or early in 2018.

3

第8段落にある形容詞 monolithic「一枚岩の=均質の」は日本人・日本社会を英語で論じる時に頻用されてきたステレオタイプの表現です。同様に用いられる語句には他にどのようなものがありますか。

Helpful Notes & Mini Quizzes

1 ▷ この「逆効果」の意味の counter productive と語義が似ている語句を記事の中から探してみましょう。
2 ▷ 金銭と関わりのない動詞 buy の意味に注意。これと対照的な意味の sell の用法も調べましょう。
3 ▷ 厚生労働省は正式な英名を The Ministry of Health, Labour, and Welfare と言うが、労働問題が論じられている時には焦点の当たっている名詞だけを残して Labor Ministry と短縮形で出ることが多い。同様に国土交通省なども、外国人観光客の急増問題の時には The Ministry of Tourism となるのに対し、新幹線網拡張などという内容の時は The Ministry of Transportation と別形で出ることに注意。
4 ▷ ここでは失職した人を「漂流する」と表していますが、このような比喩表現は突然使われているのでしょうか。それともこれを引き出すような前置きとなる比喩的表現があるのでしょうか。

Current English Composition

次の日本語を英語にしなさい。
ただし、下線を引いた部分は下線部のみを英語にしなさい。

1 <u>市場を拡大するには、買ってもらえそうな客を増加させることが重要で、それには見込み客の需要を十分に考慮し、商品の良さを詳細に説明することである。</u>
（第3段落 "a prospective employee" 参考）

_____
_____ by fully taking into account their needs and explaining advantages of the products in detail to them.

2 政府は退職者に高額の医療保障や社会保障給付を提供するが、高齢化が進んでいるのでこのような給付を受ける人の人口が増え、給付金を積み立てるために税金を払う労働者の人口は減る。<u>この税負担それ自体が経済成長の足手まといとなりうるのだ。</u>（第4段落 drag 参考）

The government provides retirees with pricey medical care and social security benefits. An aging population will mean more people collecting these benefits and fewer workers to pay the taxes that fund them. _____
_____ .

3 <u>多くの日本人は日本の会社に見られる独特の雇用形態を良いものと思ってきた。</u>年功序列賃金と経営陣と対抗できる労働組合に支えられた生涯雇用である。

_____
_____ : lifetime jobs supported by seniority-based salaries and labor unions that favored cooperation over confrontation with management.

4 いわゆる「ガラスの天井」を壊して、女性の活躍を支援するような会社は、そうでない会社よりもずっと健全な収益を知らないうちに上げているのです。

_____
_____ find themselves with much healthier bottom lines.

Chapter 11

高齢化の日本社会と社会保障

Ⅴ 経済問題

大学生の皆さんが 30 歳代の働き盛りになる頃、日本はどのような社会になっているでしょうか。高齢化が進めば、医療、介護などの社会保障にかかる費用は莫大なものになります。財政的に破綻せずにわが国の社会保障制度を持続させるためには、どうすれば良いのでしょうか。

Key Words Check

これから読む記事に登場する重要単語をチェックしましょう。
（ ）内は該当する段落番号を示しています。

infrastructure (3)

chronic (7)

commensurate (9)

asset (9)

liquidity (11)

blueprint (13)

Disaster awaits if graying Japan delays social security reforms

1 What will Japan be like 12 years from now, in the year 2030? The National Institute of Population and Social Security Research in Tokyo tried to answer that question—at least partially, anyway—in a recent report.

2 Japan's population that year will be 119.13 million, according to the report, or 8 million fewer people than in 2015. Driving that decline will be a steep increase in the number of Japanese age 75 or older, which will rise by about 7 million to 22.88 million. The report also projects that all 47 prefectures will have smaller populations by that year. In short, Japan will join the club of "super-aged" countries.

3 Such changes in the population structure will impact a broad range of areas, from economic growth, public finances and social security systems to the management of local governments and the maintenance of social infrastructure, such as roads, bridges and water supply and sewerage systems.

4 What is clear about Japan's public finances and social security programs is that unless all generations share the pain of spending cuts and an increased tax burden, the current systems will collapse. This is not a matter of waiting and seeing how things turn out.

5 The most pressing challenge is to prevent public health care and nursing care costs from ballooning so quickly. These expenses have been growing at a faster clip than the economy since the start of this century and are likely to rise even faster as 2030 approaches. Given that economic growth is a barometer of taxpayers' ability to bear financial burdens, the warning bells about the sustainability of the systems are already loud and clear.

6 Whatever shape the reforms take, one thing that cannot change is the existence of a universal health insurance system covering all citizens. Japan must not allow a considerable portion of the population to go uninsured, as has happened in the U.S. Here, private medical insurance holds the key. While public health insurance forms the base for ensuring medical services are provided across the country, private insurance can play a supplementary role that enables the country to maintain universal health care. Private insurance companies are increasingly offering policies that cover advanced medical treatments not included in public insurance.

7 Private insurance can play a huge role in nursing care, too, as it can facilitate the wider use of artificial intelligence and robot technology, which would ease chronic manpower shortages in the sector. Policymakers should take measures that enable more overseas caregivers to work in Japan. They should also revise the nursing care insurance system so that people who provide nursing care for family members at home are eligible for cash payouts.

8 Japan must also take steps to cope with the spread of dementia, whose sufferers are projected to rise to 8.3 million in 2030 from 5 million

sewerage：下水道

at a fast clip：素早
< cf. at a brisk clip

eligible：資格のある
dementia：Chapter 5 第6段落で前出。

at present. Those measures should include ramping up research into preventing and treating the disease through close partnerships with foreign governments and laboratories.

9 In financing the health insurance system, it is essential that the expense burden on each individual is commensurate with their wealth. That means using a patient's income and assets—rather than their age, as is the current practice—for determining their out-of-pocket fees.

10 Another target for reform is public pensions. First and foremost, the pension eligibility age should be raised to 70 from 65. Most major Western countries have already increased it to 67 or 68, and Japanese live longer than Westerners on average.

11 In tandem with that change should be labor market reform. Pension reforms would take hold better if systems were introduced to increase liquidity in the labor market and enable seniors to work in a more flexible manner. The environment for raising the pension eligibility age would improve if more seniors were motivated to continue working and therefore still contribute to social security.

12 The Health, Labor and Welfare Ministry plans to review the financial health of the country's public pension systems in 2019. If, during that process, the ministry embraces unrealistically high projections for economic growth and other indicators, that will only postpone reforms that are badly needed. Doing so would be an act of betrayal toward younger Japanese. The forecasts therefore need to be conservative.

13 To prevent Japan's public finances and social security programs from collapsing, Japan needs a "compass" to guide it. That compass, in this case, is a medium- to long-term blueprint for securing the necessary financial resources.

14 Relying on quick and easy ways to drum up cash will eventually only serve to exacerbate the existing distortions in the systems. Now is the time for the government to start working out a road map for the steps it has to take after the consumption tax is increased to 10% in October 2019.

(822 words)

"Disaster awaits if graying Japan delays social security reforms: Time to raise the pension eligibility age and share the health insurance burden more equally", *Nikkei Asian Review* (May 8, 2018)

Comprehension Check

1 この記事を読んで、いわゆるインフラとはどのようなものを指すのか考えなさい。

2 この記事では、日本の財政と社会保障に関する今後の課題についてどのように主張していますか。

3 この記事では、国民皆保険制度を維持するために重要なものは何であり、またそれはどのような役割を果たすと述べていますか。

Build up Your Vocabulary

1
第12段落に「厚生労働省」The Ministry of Health, Labor and Welfare が出てきます。関連して次の意味の英語表現を学習しましょう。

二院制議会

通産省

地方創生担当大臣

総務省

2
第5段落に ballooning「急速に膨らむ・増大する」という表現があります。「急に増える」の意味で使われる現在分詞形（〜ing）の語を調べましょう。

3
第7段落の manpower shortages「人手不足」という表現と関連して、以下の日本語に相当する英語表現を学習しましょう。

水不足

労働力不足

認識不足

後継者不足

4
"super-aged" countries（第2段落）との関連で以下の意味の英語表現も学習しましょう。

高齢化社会

高齢社会

脱工業化社会

Helpful Notes

1 ▷ 国立社会保障・人口問題研究所。厚生省の試験研究機関で、1996年、厚生省人口問題研究所と特殊法人社会保障研究所の統合によって設立された。

2 ▷ 共通点を持つ国の関係を club で表す例として「核兵器保有国」nuclear / atomic club（英米仏中露にインドとパキスタンが加わった）がある。

3 ▷ この "go uninsured" は、"go barefoot"「裸足でいる」などの状態の継続や、悪い意味の補語が動詞 go の後に置かれる "go bankrupt"「破産する」などと類似。"go unanswered"「願いが聞き届けられない」など、否定接頭辞 un- の付いた過去分詞もしばしば現れる。方針や政策を表す "go green"「国や企業が環境に配慮した政策を取る」なども参考。

4 ▷ chronic「慢性の」は疾患について使う形容詞で acute「急性の」の対義語である。国の経済状態や会社の業績は人間の心身状態を示す語句で比喩的に表される。Chapter 13 では、企業の消失を extinction「種の絶滅」に喩えていることを参照。

5 ▷ 各地方自治体では、要介護高齢者の在宅生活の継続、向上、及び介護する家族の経済的負担の軽減を図り、一定の要件を満たした場合に家族介護慰労金を支給しているが、金額は年額10万円程度である（支給対象者と金額は自治体により異なる）。

6 ▷ 強意語としての badly は、必ずしも「悪く、まずく」などのマイナスの意味ではないことに注意。"awfully busy" "terribly sorry" など参照。

Current English Composition

次の日本語を英語にしなさい。
ただし、下線を引いた部分は下線部のみを英語にしなさい。

1. 市民グループは地方自治体に、投票権を <u>18歳以上の日本人と外国人居住者にも広げる</u>よう要求している。（第2段落 "age 75 or older" 参考）

    The citizens' group wants local governments to expand the range of eligible voters _____ .

2. <u>福島第一原子力発電所廃炉作業にかかる費用がどんどんかさんでいるので</u>、政府は当初予定よりも長期にわたり東京電力の経営に関与することになりそうだ。
    (第5段落 "ballooning" 参考)

    The government will remain involved in the management of Tepco longer than planned because of _____ .

3. 仕事を持つ母親たちは、<u>子供を預けられる保育所の慢性的不足に加えて</u>、家庭生活とキャリアの厳しい選択に直面している。

    Working mothers are forced to make a tough choice between their families and their careers with _____ .

4. 参議院の選挙制度改革を<u>求める議員が増えている</u>。
    (第6段落 "are increasingly offering" 参考)

    _____ reform of the Upper House electoral system.

Chapter 12

日本経済の過去と未来

V 経済問題

人生にも社会にも、節目の時というものがあります。それは、過去を振り返り、現状を見つめ直し、未来への進み方を模索する格好の機会です。日本にとって2018年、2019年はそういう年です。この時期に記事では日本社会についてどのような考察と展望を示しているでしょうか。

Key Words Check

これから読む記事に登場する重要単語をチェックしましょう。
（　）内は該当する段落番号を示しています。

- resolution (1)
- consecutive (3)
- oust (4)
- feasible (8)
- monetary (11)
- unprecedented (11)
- liquid (15)
- personnel (15)
- abdication (16)

Japan should tackle New Year challenges while winds are favorable

1 Now that 2018 is in full swing, let us consider what New Year's resolutions Japan should make, and the main challenges facing the government and businesses in achieving them.

2 Goldman Sachs forecasts the world's gross domestic product will grow 4% this year, up from 3.7% in 2017. For the first time in years, the global economy is entering a new year amid largely favorable winds.

3 Japan's GDP posted a seventh consecutive quarter of growth through the July-September period, and many economists predict the growth rate for fiscal 2017, which ends in March, will be close to 2%. Workforce shortages caused by an aging and declining population have prompted companies to invest more in labor-saving technologies. Listed companies are expected to post a record combined net profit for fiscal 2017.

4 The new year will likely be less stormy on the domestic political front, too. The lower house was dissolved for a snap election only a few months ago, and there will be no upper house election until the summer of 2019. The ruling Liberal Democratic Party is to hold a presidential election this autumn, but Prime Minister Shinzo Abe has no rival who threatens to oust him as party chief.

5 In a recent speech, Christine Lagarde, managing director of the International Monetary Fund, borrowed the words of late U.S. President John F. Kennedy, saying that "the time to repair the roof is when the sun is shining." Painful reforms, in other words, should be carried out while the economy is faring well."

6 This year marks the 150th anniversary of the Meiji Restoration, a historical milestone that put Japan on track toward modernization. The past century and a half is divided into two distinct halves. The first extends from the Meiji Restoration to the Pacific War, while the second encompasses Japan's postwar reconstruction, its economic bubble and other developments down to the present day. What should be the government's first priority, particularly as the country prepares for a change in Imperial era names after the emperor steps down next year?

7 The most crucial task is to draw a blueprint of what the country's social security system and public finance should look like, with a view to coping with the advent of a super-aged society. It is a challenge comparable to constructing a modern state or rebuilding an economy, but we hope the government will face it squarely and formulate an economic policy package this summer.

8 AGE ISSUES

All of Japan's baby boomers will be 75 years or older by 2025, after which it will be even more difficult to rein in ballooning social security costs. Over the next two to three decades, as the number of those elderly keeps growing, the working-age population is set to decline. Increases in healthy life expectancy mean it is no longer feasible to maintain the current age threshold for social security programs for the elderly.

9 The number of people 65 or older as a percentage of the total work force is also growing. We suggest considering a comprehensive package of measures aimed at raising the pension eligibility age to 70 incrementally, while also making efforts to increase employment opportunities for elderly citizens.

10 The Abe government is prepared to raise the consumption tax to 10% from 8% in 2019. The problem is what to do as a follow-up. The government must devise a plan for pushing ahead with further tax hikes at a moderate but continuous pace, while also keeping an eye on whether such increases risk pushing the country back into deflation or triggering a spike in the yen's value.

11 The government will also have to be careful regarding monetary policy, which has become more closely linked with public finances than before. While U.S. and European monetary authorities are moving to wind down their unprecedented monetary easing, Bank of Japan Gov. Haruhiko Kuroda has indicated that his first priority is breaking the deflationary mindset in Japan.

12 But the BOJ must not forget to provide the market with clear signals as to what economic conditions would make the bank rethink its monetary policy, and in what order it intends to implement any policy changes.

13 The public sector alone cannot invigorate the Japanese economy. There is much that the private sector must do, too. Companies should use more of their ample cash reserves for investing in new technologies and rewarding employees.

14 It has been many years since the days when Japanese companies were churning out epoch-making products and services. In the digital age we now live in, companies must utilize both in-house and outside talent to tackle challenges nimbly and without fear of failure.

15 Creating a highly liquid labor market is a challenge for Japan. Another urgent task is to facilitate the reform of corporate labor and personnel management, and to further promote women's participation in the workforce.

16 Many major events are scheduled to take place in Japan in 2019: Emperor Akihito's abdication and a change in the country's Imperial era names, local elections across the country, an upper house election and an annual summit of the Group of 20 leading economies, with Japan holding the rotating chairmanship. Where Japan stands 10 years from now will hinge largely on whether the country can manage to tackle its various challenges ahead of these events.

(904 words)

"Japan should tackle New Year challenges while winds are favorable: Time is ripe to address such issues as labor reforms and social security spending", *Nikkei Asian Review* (January 11, 2018)

Comprehension Check

1 この記事では、日本の政治経済の動向をある統一したイメージで喩えています。それはどのようなイメージでしょうか。喩えとなっている表現を拾い上げて考察しなさい。

2 この記事では、今後の日本について政府が取り組むべき最優先課題はどのようなことだと主張していますか。

3 今後の日本社会の高齢化に対し、この記事ではどのように対処すべきだと提言していますか。

Build up Your Vocabulary

1

第6段落に明治維新 the Meiji Restoration という表現があります。関連して次の意味の英語表現を勉強しましょう。

徳川幕府の鎖国政策

戊辰戦争

五箇条の御誓文

文明開化

2

第15段落に a highly liquid labor market「流動的な労働市場」という表現があります。これと関連して次の語の意味も調べましょう。

liquefaction

liquidation

consolidation

solidarity

3

中東と欧州での移民・難民の増加や日本での外国人観光客の急増についてのニュース記事では、しばしば海と波のイメージが連続して比喩的に用いられます。実際に最近の英文ニュースを読んで、そのような例を見つけましょう。

Helpful Notes

1 ▷ 選挙戦や政策が有利に展開する状況を「追い風が吹く」と言うが、英語でも同様に "a tailwind, favorable winds" という表現を用いる。
2 ▷ 「官民一体で」「政財官」「国民と政府」"the government and the public" "cooperation between the state and the people" などの政府、業界、国民を対比させる日英の表現を参考。
3 ▷ 米国ニューヨークに本社を置く世界最大級の金融機関。投資銀行業務、証券業務、資産運用業務などを手掛ける。
4 ▷ 国際通貨基金。国連専門機関の一つで、第2次世界大戦後の世界通貨制度安定のため、自由貿易と金・ドル本位制に基づく多角的決済方式を確立し、国際的為替安定を図ることを目的として1945年に設立された。本部はワシントン。
5 ▷ Chapter 11 の第13段落で前出 "a medium- to long-term blueprint for securing the necessary financial resources"。
6 ▷ 「社内」「社外」の対比は "in-house or outside" で表される。
7 ▷ 「人事の」personnel は語尾 –nel にストレスがあること注意。会社の人事部・人事課は Human Resources（複数形）でも表される。
8 ▷ Group of 20: 世界の重要な経済・金融問題を協議する国際会議、またそのメンバーである20か国・地域を指す。メンバーは主要国首脳会議（G7）に参加する日本、アメリカ、イギリス、フランス、ドイツ、イタリア、カナダの7か国に加え、ロシア、中国、インド、韓国、インドネシア、オーストラリア、サウジアラビア、南アフリカ、トルコ、メキシコ、ブラジル、アルゼンチン、ヨーロッパ連合（EU）。会議では金融危機、財政健全化などの経済問題に加え、地球温暖化、新型ウイルス、テロ、途上国問題などについても協議される。

Current English Composition

次の日本語を英語にしなさい。
ただし、下線を引いた部分は下線部のみを英語にしなさい。

1. 14歳のプロの棋士藤井聡太は、この月曜日に、29連勝の新記録を打ち立てた。
（第3段落 "a seventh consecutive quarter" 参考）

Sota Fujii, a 14-year-old professional shogi player set _____
_____ on Monday.

2. 国連の報告によれば、日本では2025年までに20歳以下の人口が65歳以上の人口の6割になると予想されている。（第8段落 "75 years or older" 参考）

According to a U.N. report, Japan will have _____
_____ by 2025.

3. 一人だけでは職場環境を改善することはできない。
（第13段落 "The public sector alone cannot invigorate" 参考）

Chapter 13

後継者不足で中小企業の技術消失

日本のものづくりは、超一流の技術と細やかな心づかいで、世界中の信頼を勝ち取ってきました。それを支えてきたのは中小企業の人々のたゆみない努力です。ところが今、その中小企業が存続の危機に直面しています。日本の産業、経済を守るための方策が問われています。

V 経済問題

© IYO / PIXTA

Key Words Check

これから読む記事に登場する重要単語をチェックしましょう。
（　）内は該当する段落番号を示しています。

SMEs (1)

hypodermic (3)

patent (4)

retiree (9)

mass extinction (11)

overhaul (13)

Japan's 1.2 million heirless businesses at risk of closure

1 TOKYO—Some 1.27 million small and midsize businesses in Japan face the risk of closure due to a lack of successors. Already, roughly half the companies that go out of business do so despite being in the black. As more than 60% of SMEs are due to be run by managers aged 70 or older by 2025, the crisis will only intensify.

2 The government is scrambling to prevent these companies from dying en masse. Not only would a widespread die-off weaken the backbone of Japanese industry, it could also result in the loss of exclusive technology.

3 In Tokyo's Sumida district, in the shadow of the landmark Tokyo Skytree, Okano Kogyo produces ultrathin painless hypodermic needles. The metalworking company, founded in 1924, is internationally renowned for its unique technology, but Masayuki Okano, its 84-year-old chairman, is pessimistic about its future. "I'm thinking I'll close the company in about two years," Okano says with a calm suggesting he has reached a kind of understanding with the situation.

4 Okano Kogyo's manufacturing of molds and presses has helped improve technology for producing automobiles and other goods as well, and the company is in the black. But "there's no one to take over" from Okano, who says his two daughters "took a different path." Control of the company's needle manufacturing equipment will pass to medical equipment maker Terumo, which shares patents on the machinery.

5 It will be "a blow to the foundations of manufacturing if businesses with unique technology die out," says an executive at an autoparts maker that has done business with Okano.

6 Hagoromo Chalk again

Some 29,583 of Japan's small and midsize enterprises closed temporarily or permanently in 2016, according to Tokyo Shoko Research. That figure represents a steep rise from 2007's roughly 21,000. The shrinking population is increasingly leading to the closures.

7 Two years ago, the closure of Hagoromo Chalk caused grief around the world—especially among mathematicians. The 82-year-old Japanese company's tough, dustless product was considered the "Rolls Royce" of chalk, but its president, Takayasu Watanabe, opted to shut down because he had no successor.

8 "We received a flood of faxes and nonstop telephone calls, and could hardly keep up with orders," Watanabe said in an interview about the response to his announcement. With nobody to pass the baton to, he shipped the remaining chalk-producing machines to South Korea.

9 In 2015, the largest portion of small and midsize business managers were between the ages of 65 and 69, says the Ministry of Economy, Trade and Industry. Such managers retire on average at 70, and in 2025, about 2.45 million—at least 60%—will be at retirement age. Some 1.27 million, or about half the number of retirees-to-be, said in a METI survey they had not appointed a successor. About 70% of sole proprietors age 60 or older said their business would not continue after them. "A period is approaching in which many businesses will close," says one METI official. "The next decade will be crucial."

10 Businesses folding after losing money continuously and reaching their financial limit "can help renew the industry," says Professor Iichiro Uesugi of Hitotsubashi University's Institute of Economic Research. "But when a highly productive, profitable business closes, it lowers the economy's overall performance."

11 Moving urgently

If left unchecked, such closures could rob Japan of about 6.5 million jobs and 22 trillion yen ($194 billion) in gross domestic product by 2025, according to METI's internal calculations. Businesses passed on across generations also strongly tend to increase profitability and sales. Japan's government intends to churn out policy over the next half decade or so to avoid a mass extinction.

12 To spur succession arrangements to come together quickly, Tokyo will need to make full use of tax codes, financial mechanisms and budgetary measures. Right now, managers taking on a business from a relative can defer payment of inheritance taxes and gift taxes, for instance. But they can only do so if they keep on at least 80% of employees, so that provision has been criticized for being hard to take advantage of.

13 The government plans to drastically overhaul such areas, as well as lighten the tax burden small to midsize business managers face from mergers and acquisitions. There is also plenty of room for the government to link up with banks and other institutions to expand support programs, such as low-interest loans to encourage business heirs to invest actively.

14 A wider net

Some businesses are finding successors outside company walls. At Hiroshima's Miyakehonten, the veteran brewer of Sempuku brand sake, President Miyake Kiyotsugu brought in a staffer from the Japan Human Resources agency to help.

15 Miyake's son, the company heir, was still in his 20s. It would be faster "to take in someone from outside who can carry on the medium-term management plan," Miyake argued, waving off internal inclinations for a more cautious approach. The president also figured casting a wider net could help the business rack its brains for a way to sell to young people, who are increasingly drifting away from sake.

16 The government aims to increase outside appointments by lightening regulations on second and side businesses. Also, specialists at chambers of commerce and other bodies nationwide have consulted with managers to help find successors in as many as 800 cases. That figure is planned to grow to 2,000 cases annually in five years, though this is still a drop in the bucket given the over 1 million businesses in need of successors.

17 To address the problem on a larger scale, many say Japan should have a market for small-scale mergers and acquisitions so investors can more easily approach such enterprises. France, for instance, has a nationwide online database of information on businesses looking to sell.

18 Such a market would make it easier for Asian investors to get involved as well. Overseas help is certainly an option if it helps stave off mass closures and keeps Japan's industry healthy.

(1015 words)

stave off：遅らせる、防ぐ

"Japan's 1.2 million heirless businesses at risk of closure: With 'Rolls Royce' of chalk already gone, country could lose key technologies" by Takashi Tsuji, *Nikkei Asian Review* (October 9, 2017)

Comprehension Check

1 本記事では、中小企業の倒産を表す語をある統一したイメージでたとえています。どのようなイメージか、たとえとなっている表現を拾い上げて考察しなさい。

2 第2段落に見られる "exclusive technology" とはどのようなものですか。

3 本記事では、優れた中小企業の廃業・倒産は日本経済にどのような影響をもたらすと述べていますか。

Build up Your Vocabulary

1

第2段落に die-off「大量死」という表現があります。大量、完全、完了の意味は副詞 off, out, up などを付けて強調されます。次の意味を英語で表しましょう。

種を全滅させる

ミルクを全部飲み干す

グラスを満杯にする

全面戦争

丸損（完全な損失）

2

第13段落に mergers and acquisitions「企業の合併買収」という表現があります。関連して次の意味の英語表現を勉強しましょう。

繊維業界

企業の系列

上場企業

終身雇用

3

第11段落に「絶滅」extinction という語があります。これと関連して種の絶滅に関する以下の意味の英語表現を学習しましょう。

絶滅危惧種

脆弱種

生息地

地球温暖化

Helpful Notes

1 ▷ "Not only A but also B" の対比構文にはヴァリエーションが多く、only の代わりに just, merely, simply が使われ、接続詞 but を使わずに文尾に too を置く形もある。最近頻出するのは It's not A．B…と第1要素の後で文が終わり、対比される B は次の文で導入される形で、これを "Not only A but also B" の意味で取ることが肝要である。

2 ▷ 接頭辞 hypo-「〜の下の、足りない」の対義は hyper-「〜の上の、過剰の」で、hyper-activity「(子供の)運動過多」、hypertension「高血圧」などが頻用される。

3 ▷ "名詞 +to be" は「〜になる人」の意。"a mother-to-be"「妊婦」は "an expectant mother" とも言う。Chapter 10「生涯雇用の消失」第3段落の "a prospective employee" も参照。

4 ▷ 植杉威一郎氏は一橋大学経済研究所教授。専門分野は企業金融、中小企業、日本経済。

5 ▷ the tax burden の後に関係詞 which を補うと理解しやすい。

6 ▷ 動詞 brew「(ビールや日本酒などを)醸造する」て、ウィスキーや焼酎などを「蒸留する」は distill で表す。醸造所、蒸留所は brewery, distillery と言う。

7 ▷ town-wide / citywide「町中に」worldwide「世界中に」planet-wide「惑星中に＝地球全体に」など参考。Chapter 6, p. 35, Chapter 7, p. 40 で前出。

Current English Composition

次の日本語を英語にしなさい。
ただし、下線を引いた部分は下線部のみを英語にしなさい。

1 最近は和菓子の人気が世界中で高まっている。（第3段落 "is internationally renowned for" 参考）

2 日本が開国すると、たくさんの外国語の言葉が洪水のように入ってきて、国の近代化を助けた。（第8段落 "a flood of faxes" 参考）

When Japan reopened to trade and travel, _____
_____ .

3 日本の鉄道には危険な踏切がたくさんあるが、ここ何年も、多くが手つかずのままにされている。（第11段落 "left unchecked," 参考）

Many of Japan's hazardous railroad crossings _____
_____ .

4 当局によると、日韓首脳は自由貿易協定（FTA）締結に向けての公式の交渉を始めるということだ。（第12段落 "Tokyo will need to make full use of tax codes" 参考）

_____ toward establishing an FTA, the officials said.

Chapter 14

おもてなしの心

あの五輪招致のプレゼンテーションで世界的に脚光を浴びた日本の「おもてなし」。おもてなし文化を誇りに思う人は多いようですが、これは外国人が望むものでしょうか。誇るべきものなのでしょうか。もてなす側ともてなされる側、双方の気持ちについてあらためて考えてみましょう。

VI 外国人と日本人

© Fast&Slow / PIXTA

Key Words Check

これから読む記事に登場する重要単語をチェックしましょう。
（ ）内は該当する段落番号を示しています。

- presumption (1)
- brag (2)
- implicit (2)
- snobbery (4)
- solicitous (4)
- refutation (6)
- influx (9)
- tenet (10)
- castigate (11)

Omotenashi comes up short on humility

1 A Japanese friend who used to travel a lot for work told me of a funny thing that once happened to her in a Tokyo hotel. She was checking in when a bellhop came up and, without saying anything, picked up her bag. She resented the presumption and tried to yank it out of his hand. A silent tug of war ensued.

2 The bellhop wasn't being rude or, for that matter, particularly Japanese. He was just operating according to instructions. My friend told me this story to illustrate her reaction to the increased currency of the word *omotenashi*, which, ever since Tokyo won the right to hold the 2020 Olympic Games, is used to describe the Japanese style of hospitality and, when it's covered by the media, a source of national pride. To my friend, omotenashi is not something you talk about, much less brag over. There's something arrogant about the idea that one's hospitality is superior to another's, which was the message implicit in the Olympic bid campaign.

3 Though I know other Japanese people who feel the same way as my friend, the media usually go to non-Japanese if they want an opinion about omotenashi, since it is foreign visitors who are meant to be impressed by yet another unique quality of Japanese culture.

4 Last January, the economic magazine Toyo Keizai interviewed Mohamed Omer Abdin, a Sudanese who works at the Tokyo University of Foreign Studies. In the piece, Abdin calls omotenashi "Japanese snobbery." He isn't talking about the over-solicitous service offered by the bellhop, but rather the high-minded attitude contained in the word. He cites an NHK survey from 2013 that found 67 percent of respondents thought "Japanese people possess excellent characters compared to other countries." He found this self-praise contradictory, given that the ostensible reason for omotenashi is to treat guests in a special way, but the survey suggests that the respondents "reject the good features of other countries."

5 The usual reaction to such comments is that because the person is not Japanese he or she doesn't fully understand the situation, which is often true but a pointless observation given the subject at hand. If the individual who is receiving the benefits of omotenashi finds them not beneficial, then something must be wrong. Abdin believes that the associated interaction is skewed. In the dynamic of omotenashi, the giver of hospitality knows what is best for the guest and does not consider alternatives. The wishes of the guest are not important, because the idea is to provide "service even when it isn't asked for."

6 Cultural insensitivity aside, the focus on omotenashi actually distracts from its main purpose, which, as the Olympic bid illustrated, is to draw foreign visitors to Japan. According to David Atkinson, a former analyst for Salomon Brothers and Goldman Sachs who has become a kind of one-man refutation of the virtues of omotenashi, while hospitality is appreciated by non-Japanese, it is not what they come for. They come to see things, and the Japanese tourist industry mostly disregards this aspect.

→ 📖 1

→ 📖 2

→ 📖 3

ostensible：表向きの、見かけの。Chapter 10 第 2 段落 "the part they were ostensibly hired to serve" 参照。

skewed：ゆがんだ、もてなす側のみに傾いた

Salomon Brothers：ソロモン・ブラザーズは 1910 年に設立されたアメリカの大手投資銀行・証券会社。
Goldman Sachs：アメリカ、ニューヨー

7 In a Sept. 20 article on the financial page of the Asahi Shimbun, Atkinson, who currently heads a 300-year-old company that oversees the preservation of temples and other historical buildings, contends that Japan needs as many tourists as possible in order to achieve growth, because growth is impossible without an increase in population. Since Japan is unwilling to accept permanent immigrants, it needs to attract more "temporary immigrants," meaning tourists.

8 But the tourism sector hasn't really done enough research into what foreign visitors are looking for. They only talk about omotenashi. The government loves to designate things and places as important cultural assets, but they don't promote those assets in ways that appeal to foreigners. Atkinson finds most of the historical sightseeing spots in Japan lacking in value-added features that would make them attractive to non-Japanese. The U.K. invests the equivalent of ¥50 billion a year in the repair and maintenance of its national treasures, and tourism accounts for 9 percent of its GDP. Japan invests ¥8.1 billion, and tourism accounts for 2 percent of GDP.

9 It's true that foreign tourism is on the rise in Japan, but that's because of the large influx of Chinese, who come to shop, not to sightsee. Kyoto, considered the jewel of Japanese cities, receives almost 2 million foreign visitors a year. Paris gets 15 million, and while the French capital has the advantage of being in the middle of Europe, Atkinson thinks Kyoto could boost its numbers if it endeavored to find out what foreigners want to do there.

10 He elaborated on this idea in a conversation with Hitotsubashi University professor Yoko Ishikura in the Harvard Business Review in June, saying that Kyoto's leaders have an "unshakeable belief" that theirs is "the best tourist city in the world," a smug misconception "fed by the media." This is the problem with omotenashi, whose tenet is not that the customer is always right, but rather that the service provider knows what's best for the customer. He says this way of thinking extends to Japanese craftsmanship, manufacturing and even to some traditional pastimes, like tea ceremony, which is not about the guest, but rather about the host. The guest's role is to "appreciate the host's fine taste." What the guest wants is unimportant.

11 Atkinson speaks from a position of authority, and not just because he is a long-term resident of Japan whose interest in the country is wide-ranging. It was Atkinson who revealed the extent of the bad credit (*furyō saiken*) that brought down the Japanese economy in the 1990s. When the media reported that he had calculated the debt to be ¥20 trillion, he was castigated by the financial community, which only conveys to investors what it wants them to know. Actually, the debt was even worse, but the point is that omotenashi even extends to the banking industry. As in my friend's case, it won't let you alone.

(1010 words)

Comprehension Check

1 第3段落末尾の "…it is foreign visitors who are meant to be impressed by yet another unique quality of Japanese culture." の意味を、yet another に注意しながら説明しなさい。

2 第4段落の末尾の文に "He found this self-praise contradictory," とありますが、どういうところが "contradictory" なのか、わかりやすく説明しなさい。

3 本記事の最終文、"As in my friend's case, it won't let you alone." により筆者が主張しようとしていることを、記事全体の内容をふまえて説明しなさい。

Build up Your Vocabulary

1

本記事で論じられている「おもてなし」という言葉のように、以下の日本文化に特有の語は、どのような英語表現で表せるでしょうか。

忖度（そんたく）する

根回し

もったいない

思いやり

2

第 10 段落で茶席の作法のことが言及されています。これと関連して日本の伝統芸能・文化を表す英語表現を勉強しましょう。

茶道

華道

書道

水墨画

禅寺

枯山水庭園

わび（侘び）

3

和食ブームと言われています。日本語から既に英語化された料理名もありますが、次の食べ物を説明する短い英語の文を考えましょう。

ラーメン

焼き鳥

（回転）寿司

お好み焼き

Helpful Notes

1 ▷ この部分 "a tug of war" が比喩であり、かつ実際に引っ張り合っているのが面白いところ。When Greek meets Greek, then comes the tug of war.「両雄相まみえれば激しく渡り合う」Chapter 4 第 14 段落参照。

2 ▷ "yet another burden on educators" Chapter 7 第 13 段落および "the media has advanced yet another new term" Chapter 8 第 1 段落参照。

3 ▷ 『東洋経済』では 2015 年 1 月 13 日の「『おもてなし』礼賛は日本の思い上がりだ——観光立国を名乗る前にやるべきこと」と題する記事で、モハメド・オマル・アブディン氏へのインタビュー内容を記している。(http://toyokeizai.net/articles/-/57728?page=2)

4 ▷ この数値は宿泊人数を指しており、2016 年には 318 万人に増えた。

5 ▷ この about の使い方に注意。「何が大事か、目指している事、今取り組んでいる仕事」などを表す。

6 ▷ この段落に書いてあることは、例えば書店での品揃えにも反映されている。茶席ての客としての作法を説くガイドブックが圧倒的に多い。

Current English Composition

次の日本語を英語にしなさい。
ただし、下線を引いた部分は下線部のみを英語にしなさい。

1 新しい大統領は 86% という驚くほど高い支持率を誇っているが、彼の政治感覚はどこかおかしい。(第 2 段落 "There's something arrogant about" 参考)

The new president enjoys a stunningly high approval rating of 86%, but _____
_____ .

2 第 188 回特別国会で、衆参両院で総理大臣を指名する選挙が行われ、安倍晋三が第 97 代の総理大臣となった。(第 8 段落 "to designate things" 参考)

During the 188th special session of the Diet, _____
_____
_____ , and Shinzo Abe became the 97th Prime Minister.

3 増加しつつある不法移民の流入が、国境を超えるテロと麻薬の流通に関する懸念を増大させている。(第 9 段落 "the large influx of Chinese" 参考)

_____ has raised concerns relating to cross-border terrorism and distribution of drugs.

4 日本人は、会話というものはそれぞれの人の考えを交換するためのものだということをよく思い出すべきです。

The Japanese need to remind themselves _____
_____ .

Chapter 15

移民を受け入れるか

日本の人口は既に減少に転じました。高齢者が増える一方、将来働き手となる子供の数も減っています。労働力不足解決の一手段は移民受け入れですが、これは可能でしょうか。

Key Words Check

これから読む記事に登場する重要単語をチェックしましょう。
（　）内は該当する段落番号を示しています。

- panacea (2)
- depopulation (6)
- stern (7)
- shibboleth (7)
- culprit (9)
- moribund (11)
- intermarriage (11)

Will Japan be a country that welcomes all?

1 "A nation of immigrants." Japan? The leading proponent of that vision has been Hidenori Sakanaka, former head of the Tokyo Immigration Bureau, current executive director of the private think tank he founded in 2007, the Japan Immigration Policy Institute.

2 His was long a voice in the wilderness as he called on Japan to welcome 10 million immigrants by 2050. In his writing, most recently a 2012 book titled "Jinko Hokai to Imin Kakumei" ("Population Breakdown and the Immigrant Revolution"), his irrepressible enthusiasm comes through in a partiality for words like "utopia" and "panacea." The problems his "revolution" would address are glaring. No nation, let alone an economic superpower, has ever faced population aging and population decline at anything like Japan's current pace. An influx of immigrants would repopulate, rejuvenate and globalize a naturally inward-looking country grown of late lethargic, complacent and old.

3 The trouble is, Japan is shy. Foreign faces, foreign languages, foreign ways make it nervous, and Sakanaka's call has generally been dismissed as quixotic.

4 Then in February, the government's Council on Economic and Fiscal Policy reportedly began discussing a plan to admit 200,000 foreigners a year. Even if still a mere talking point, it has never been even that before, this high up in official ranks. Is "a nation of immigrants" on the horizon?

5 The monthly Sapio, in its June edition, takes up the issue at some length. Is it happening? Should it happen? If so, at what pace, on what terms? If not, what are the alternatives?

6 To take the last question first, the most obvious alternative is a smaller, less competitive, less frenetic Japan, seen not as an admission of defeat but as the sensible pursuit of the good life. Arguing the case for Sapio is economic journalist Takuro Morinaga, who notes that in the 1920s Japan's population was half what is now without anyone losing sleep about underpopulation. Let depopulation take its course, he urges. Fewer people will mean fewer crowds, less pressure, more leisure. More originality too, maybe, as Japan withdraws from the competition-driven globalized rat race and turns inward in the best sense of the word, concentrating on those idiosyncratic creations whose worldwide appeal spans the modern age, from 19th-century Japanese art to 21st-century *kawaii* (cute) culture. Let Japan, says Morinaga, "be a nation of 100 million artists"—or even 87 million, since that is what the population is projected to fall to by 2060, down from a 2005 peak of 127.8 million and 126.98 million today.

7 Taking a sterner line is opposition Diet representative and former Tokyo Gov. Shintaro Ishihara, derided and extolled as a leading spokesman for the arch-conservative and xenophobic side of the Japanese character who here, however, surprises, declaring himself an eager supporter of drastically increased immigration. "Cute," one senses, is not for him. "Population is strength," he tells Sapio. "If our population continues to decline like this, inevitably our national strength will decline. I've been saying for more than 10 years that we need immigrants." He debunks a shibboleth dear to the right, that the Japanese are "one race." "That's a mistaken perception," he says, and goes on to trace Japan's ethnic roots all over Asia and Oceania.

8 Journalist Yoshiko Sakurai is another prominent member of the patriotic intelligentsia who claims long-standing recognition of the need for immigrants—though she does confess to a certain wariness. Look at the U.S., she writes in her contribution to Sapio's package. Here is a country that, though "a nation of immigrants," having been founded by immigrants, nonetheless remained until very recently predominantly WASP (white Anglo-Saxon protestant), with all the virtues she says that implies: self-reliance, freedom, respect for human rights and a confidence in those same values that made the U.S. their global champion (for better and for worse, a critic might add). Immigration en masse, some of it illegal, altered the national character, Sakurai writes, diluting the native idealism with coarser, more material concerns closer to home, an evolution reflected in President Barack Obama's declaration last September, with reference to the carnage in Syria, that "America is not the world's policeman."

9 Japan too has a distinct national character, Sakurai asserts, and though very different from America's, it too might be in danger of dilution by uncontrolled immigration. Japan's native virtues, she writes, are "kindness, sympathy, generosity and virtue," rooted in, she says, the religious and cultural institution of a royal family dating back (mythologically if not historically) to the nation's misty beginnings. Notorious outbursts of anti-Korean "hate speech" last fall, she says, disgrace those virtues and show how far Japan has already fallen, even without immigration, modern life itself perhaps being the culprit. So immigration by all means, she says—"providing immigrants obey the rules of, and assimilate into, Japanese society." Otherwise, "Japan could cease to be Japan."

10 Back and forth go the arguments—philosophical, economic and street-level, the latter including concerns about things such as noise, scofflawry and an uncomfortable feeling, expressed by some in neighborhoods where foreigners congregate, of being an outsider in your own country. Recently Toyo Keizai magazine noted a mismatch between jobs going begging, mainly in and around the construction field, and jobs Japanese job-seekers tend to want—mostly office jobs. Perhaps immigrant workers could fill the gap? Bad idea, countered Shukan Economist. Immigration may solve some problems, but only to cause others—the education of foreign children, the possible welfare needs of foreign parents, the policing of unassimilated foreign communities—for which Japan is ill equipped. Better, says Shukan Economist, to mobilize women and willing retirees. Besides, it adds, Japan's Asian neighbors face their own demographic problems. Can Japan afford to grow dependent on other countries' surplus labor?

11 In a 2005 book titled "Nyukan Senki" ("Immigration Battle Diary"), Sakanaka imagined Japan circa 2050, fully evolved into an "immigrant nation," more at ease in its cosmopolitanism than even the U.S. "melting pot" is today. Immigrants comprise 20 percent of Japan's 120 million population. Filipinos staff the nursing homes, Indians and Chinese the IT industry and Southeast Asians the currently moribund agricultural sector. Harmony reigns, intermarriage flourishes—eventually the very idea of race fades from human consciousness as bloodlines fuse and surviving racial characteristics cease to matter.

12 Is that Japan's future? Or should the last word go to a skeptical German official quoted by Morinaga in his Sapio article: "Germany had so many problems (with Turkish guest workers brought in during the 1960s to relieve a labor shortage). Why would Japan want to go that route?" (1100 words)

Comprehension Check

1 本記事では日本を繰り返し病人あるいは老人にたとえているようです。それらの言い回しを抜き出しなさい。

2 日本の人口減少問題の解決策として、本記事では移民を受け入れるという方法以外の案も紹介されています。それはどのような案か、まとめなさい。

3 この記事で紹介された、日本の移民受け入れを容認する意見をまとめなさい。

Build up Your Vocabulary

1
第11段落に「死に体の、活力を失った」の意のmoribundという比喩的意味の形容詞があります。これと関連して、人の状態を表す原義から一般的意味を発達させた形容詞を調べましょう。

2
第6段落に "a smaller, less competitive, less frenetic Japan" と国名に不定冠詞 a が付いています。人名や国名などの固有名詞が形容詞で修飾されて、一時的な状態、空想上、過去や未来を想定する場合などに冠詞 a が付き、関係節で修飾されている場合にしばしば定冠詞 the が付きます。以下の日本語を英語で表しましょう。

アニメの中で描かれた日本は、本当の日本ではない。

「お早う」と、ジャクソン氏は皮肉な調子で言った。

慌てたクリントン大統領は、「本心からそう言ったのではない」と言った。

3
第7段落に xenophobic「外国人嫌い・外人恐怖症」という言葉があります。この語尾 –phobic は「～恐怖症・嫌い」を意味する形容詞形成語尾で、対応する名詞形は –phobia です。これらの語尾を持つ表現を集めましょう。

Helpful Notes

1 ▷ （洗礼者ヨハネが荒野でメシアの到来を呼ばわったことから）荒野に叫ぶ声、世に入れられない改革者の叫び。新約聖書マタイ伝3章3節より。この文が His was で始まるのは、名詞 voice を述部で in the wilderness と連続させて、聖書からの引喩をはっきりさせるため。
2 ▷ Chapter 3, p. 19 economic power 参照。
3 ▷ Chapter 14, p. 85 では、中国人観光客の激増について使われている。
4 ▷ 「空想的な、現実離れした」スペインの小説、セルバンテスの『ドン・キホーテ』の登場人物名から。ツルゲーネフの『ハムレットとドン・キホーテ』では、前者を懐疑主義者で行動できないタイプ、後者を理想主義者で失敗ばかりする人の典型として捉える。
5 ▷ 経済財政諮問会議は内閣府に設置された合議制の機関で、経済財政政策に関し、内閣総理大臣のリーダーシップを十全に発揮させるとともに、関係国務大臣や有識者議員等の意見を十分に政策形成に反映させることを目的としている。

Current English Composition

次の日本語を英語にしなさい。
ただし、下線を引いた部分は下線部のみを英語にしなさい。

1 外国人は日本に到着すると、顔写真を撮られて、その同じ機械で指紋もスキャンされる。

2 彼の運命は開拓者の運命だった。次の世代の人々に道を開きながら、彼自身は自分の世代の中に閉じ込められていた。（第2段落 "His was..." 参考）

_____ . He cleared ground for the next generation but remained imprisoned within his own.

3 ソニー製品はかつて機械ハードウェアの世界基準であった。そこが日本の制作者達の得意分野だった。しかし今はソフトウェアの時代である。（第6段落 that is what... 参考）

Sony used to be a global standard in the hardware era. _____ . But now it's a software era.

4 日本は年末のこの時期になると、国中ではないにしても、大都市などではまるでキリスト教の国にいるように思えるだろう。（第9段落 if not... 参考）

At this time of year, _____ .

■■■ **著者略歴** ■■■

渡辺秀樹（わたなべ　ひでき）
関西外国語大学外国語学部英米語学科 教授
東京大学大学院博士課程中退、文学博士（千葉大学 2003 年）。
専門は英語史、辞書論、古英詩解釈、英詩メタファー研究。
1994 年以来、日本の時事問題記事を集めた英語リーディング用の教科書を 12 冊編集刊行。

大森文子（おおもり　あやこ）
大阪大学言語文化研究科 教授
大阪大学文学部博士課程中退、文学博士（大阪大学 2012 年）。
専門は認知言語学、日英短詩形作品研究、メタファー研究。
英語リーディング教科書 *Eco-Friendly Japan*（共編）で 2008 年大阪大学共通教育賞受賞。

本書に収録された練習問題と解答は、英文記事の出典元であるジャパンタイムズ及びその寄稿者ならびに *Nikkei Asian Review* 及びその寄稿者とは一切関係ございません。

Advanced Reading Word to Word: Various Social Issues
ニュースメディアで読み解く現代日本

2019 年 4 月 10 日　初版第 1 刷発行
2024 年 4 月 10 日　第 2 版第 3 刷発行

編 著 者　渡辺秀樹／大森文子

発 行 者　森　信久

発 行 所　株式会社　松 柏 社
　　　　　〒102-0072　東京都千代田区飯田橋 1-6-1
　　　　　TEL　03 (3230) 4813（代表）
　　　　　FAX　03 (3230) 4857
　　　　　http://www.shohakusha.com
　　　　　e-mail: info@shohakusha.com

装　　幀　小島トシノブ（NONdesign）
本文レイアウト　一柳　茂（株式会社クリエーターズユニオン）
印刷・製本　日経印刷株式会社
ISBN978-4-88198-752-0
略号＝752
Copyright © 2019 Hideki Watanabe & Ayako Omori

本書を無断で複写・複製することを禁じます。
落丁・乱丁は送料小社負担にてお取り替え致します。